SHAPERS AND FOUNDERS

SHAPERS AND FOUNDERS

THE UNTOLD STORIES OF ASIA'S EXTRAORDINARY OWNER-CEOs

McKinsey & Company

GAUTAM KUMRA · CHERYL LIM
JOYDEEP SENGUPTA

WILEY

Published by John Wiley & Sons, Inc., Hoboken, New Jersey.

For general information on our other products and services or for technical support, please contact our Customer Care Department within the United States at (800) 762-2974, outside the United States at (317) 572-3993 or fax (317) 572-4002.

Wiley also publishes its books in a variety of electronic formats. Some content that appears in print may not be available in electronic formats. For more information about Wiley products, visit our web site at www.wiley.com.

Library of Congress Cataloging-in-Publication Data is Available:

ISBN 9781394423804 (Cloth)
ISBN 9781394423811 (ePub)
ISBN 9781394423828 (ePDF)

Cover Design: Wiley
Cover Images: Yan/stock.adobe.com, Govan/stock.adobe.com, Dmitry Rukhlenko/stock.adobe.com, Luciano Mortula-LGM/stock.adobe.com, efired/stock.adobe.com, anekoho/stock.adobe.com, Travel man/stock.adobe.com, natalya2015/stock.adobe.com, SNEHIT PHOTO/stock.adobe.com, coward_lion/stock.adobe.com, Oleksandr Dibrova/stock.adobe.com
Author Photos: Courtesy of the Authors

Printed and bound by CPI Group (UK) Ltd, Croydon, CR0 4YY
C9781394423804_210726

Contents

Introduction

This book exists because of a question and a unique answer.

The question: what is it about the leadership mindset of extraordinary Asian founders that causes them to create greater value than any other form of business?

The authors were uniquely positioned to answer it. Across our careers we have worked with founders and have always been intrigued and educated by their thought processes: the way they think about risk, talent, innovation, mission, strategy, and scaling. We have seen firsthand the extraordinary results that come from their methods, and have long believed in the value of codifying their approaches into a systematic examination of what they do and why it works.

And the answer we came up with brought deeper insights through detailed firsthand interviews with select founders, who have never previously been interviewed collectively with this degree of detail, honesty, and reach. We sought them out, spoke to them at length, asked them how they work, and then brought their insights together into this book.

In our development work with CEOs through the McKinsey Center for CEO Excellence (MCCE, which the authors founded)[1] we sensed that, while all successful CEOs follow a set of mindsets and beliefs, there was a clear distinction between the approach of professional CEOs and that of extraordinary founders or owner-CEOs. We felt there was value in a deeper examination.

We want to acknowledge from the start that this is a chronicle of extraordinary success stories. We interviewed outliers, the best in their field, and it would be wrong to consider them representative of all founder- or owner-led companies. Plenty of people who own and run businesses get it wrong; they are not in these pages.

But these insights matter because they help to decode the DNA of people who have done remarkable things at scale. They provide us with useful lessons: everyone from the professional CEO to the business student can gain something from what they have to tell us.

Asia's Era

Let's start with where they are.

This is Asia's era. Asia today enjoys the world's most dynamic growth, whether it's in gross domestic product (GDP), trade flows, corporate earnings, or new patent generation. This is where the economic momentum is, where innovation thrives, where companies with new ideas can scale the fastest.

At a fractious time for geopolitics and trade, one of the few things we can say with certainty is that Asia's position in the world order is likely to become more entrenched. Trade might be disrupted between continental blocs, but it is unlikely to be stalled within Asia, for this is where connectivity resides. Intra-Asian trade is rising at a faster rate than global trade; intra-regional trade comprised nearly 60% of Asia's total exports in 2024.[2] Asia will only matter more to the world in the years ahead.

In many respects, it is already the world's main economic story. The last 50 years have brought about a transformation in Asia's standing in the world economy, and today the continent frequently represents a global majority, or will soon do so, as shown in Figure I.1. Today Asia

Figure I.1 Asia Is Becoming the World's New "Majority"

Source: IMF; UN Comtrade; UNESCO; National Science Foundation; WIPO; Energy Institute Statistical Review of World Energy; Bloomberg New Energy Finance; IRENA; IHS Markit; McKinsey Global Institute analysis.

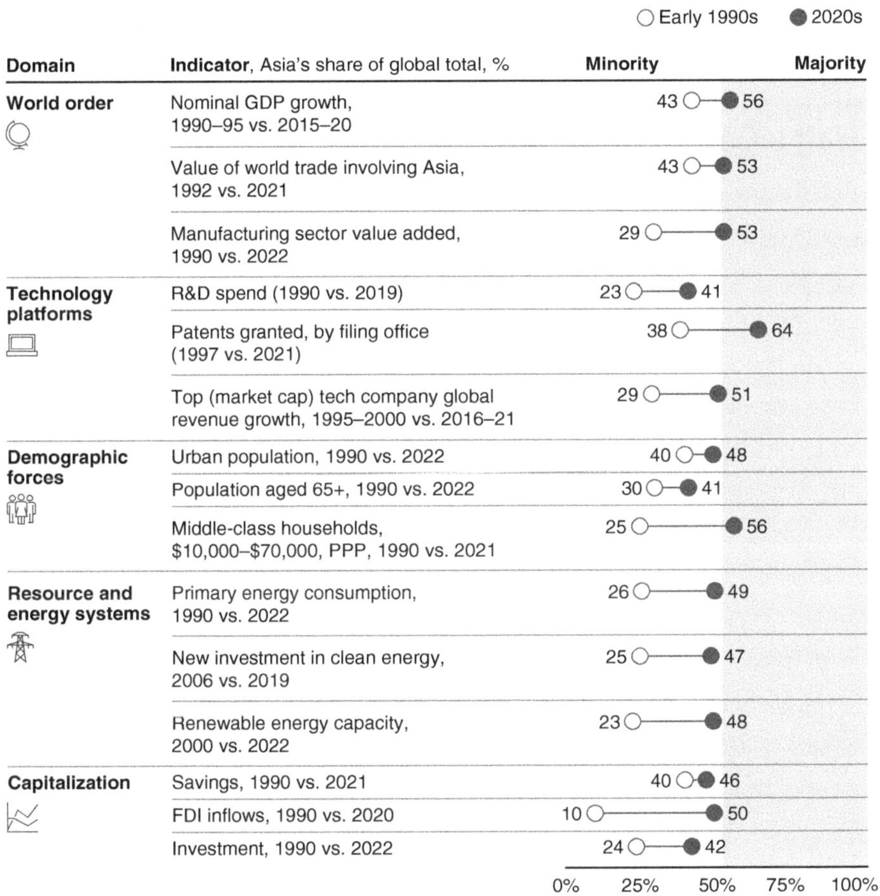

accounts for 56% of nominal global GDP growth; 53% of world trade involves it. Not only does Asia house a comfortable majority of the world's population but also 48% of its urban population and 56% of all middle-class households.[3]

Asia has also driven to a strong position in classical measures of innovation. Asia already has the largest single slice of world-class patents in electrification and renewables, the future of mobility, Web3, and advanced connectivity; it is significant in all forms of artificial intelligence, immersive-reality technologies, trust architectures and digital identity, and space technology.

Half a Century of Momentum

Asia's economic story since 1980 is replete with headline numbers. China's per capita GDP has grown five times faster than that of the United States in that time frame. South Korea's economy grew 28 times over and ASEAN[4] collective GDP, more than 12-fold.

Behind the economic tailwind is the demographic one. Asia's combined population was 2.1 billion in 1980; it crossed 4.2 billion in 2024, which means the addition of more than two billion potential consumers, workers, and creators in 44 years. Each of India and China individually has a population bigger than that of North America and Europe combined. Western populations grew only 20–25% in that same period when Asia's were doubling. So Asia's entrepreneurs have enjoyed a powerful demographic engine the West has not.

Just as important as the scale of that population is the growing wealth within it. The average Asian per capita income rose 10–25 times during that period, depending on the location, compared to three to four times in the United States and Europe. This compression of prosperity has two clear impacts: available wealth to be spent or invested, with a consequent boost to every sector from consumer goods to financial services, and an underpinning of the region's entrepreneurial urgency with each generation expecting a higher baseline than the one before.

Who's Driving Value Creation?

Founder-led companies, we have learned, produce more value than any peer group. They are the best value-creators in the most vibrant region in the world. Here's the proof.

If we study the global rolling top 5,000 companies since 2000 by market capitalization,[5] we observe a swift evolution. In 2000–2002, Asia accounted for 14% of the global market capitalization; by 2022–2024 it was 27%. Asian companies represent more than 30% (US$24 trillion) of the global total market capitalization value creation (US$78 trillion) among top companies over this approximate 25-year period. Out of that US$24 trillion, the top 10% of companies (~295) accounted for 58% (US$14 trillion) of market capitalization value creation.

And something very interesting happens when we further filter Asia's top 10% (~295). We learn that entrepreneur-led businesses drive disproportionate value. They account for ~45% of Asia's value creation among top companies (see "Our Method"). They are the true engine of growth.

To complement our own insights from serving these individuals, we interviewed 30 of these leaders from all over the Asia Pacific region, asking them to share their reflections on what made them successful.

The sample of founders and owners we engaged covers multiple countries, nations, and sectors. They range from third- or fourth-generation owner-CEOs of leading multinationals to first-generation founders of daring new businesses in frontier economies. Where they have a story we think the reader needs to hear, we have sought other voices to share, including private equity names who are founders in their own right but also have a front-row view of how the businesses they invest in are driven by founder-entrepreneurs.[6]

Our Method

Figure I.2 explains how we created our universe of Asia's most value-creating companies. Market capitalization is our key identifier for value creation, since it reflects the value delivered to the market over the long-term. There are other useful ways to assess financial performance – economic profit, return on invested capital (ROIC) – but many of the companies in this book are making substantial investments with a focus on long-term goals, even nation building. Market cap captures that value creation better than profit or ROIC.

The founder-entrepreneur group – those led by founder-entrepreneurs or their family or where a significant share of ownership or influence is held by the original business founder, their family, or employees – is distinct from two other constituencies. Those are companies whose largest shareholder or voting power falls into one of two camps: institutional investors, or state-owned enterprises, a powerful bloc in Asia. We chose to focus on the first group rather than the others to see how value creation by founder-led companies compared to other forms of ownership.

The universe of about 130 founder-led companies that results from these filters shows an outsized performance compared to the universe of 295 that includes all kinds of businesses. They account for nearly half of

We also spoke to many colleagues who have insights into other founder-led companies to gain knowledge, validate our observations, and to provide input into our thinking.

This body of unique material enables us to trace common traits between these leaders from which other aspiring business leaders can learn. The leaders are too complex, individual, and gifted for us to suggest we can create a recipe to become like them. But we can do our best to understand their mindsets and behaviors.

total value creation, 45% as measured by growth in market capitalization, while state-owned enterprises contribute just 32% of the value growth and institutionally-owned just 23%.

Figure I.2 Methodology Used to Identify Asia's Most Value-Creating Companies

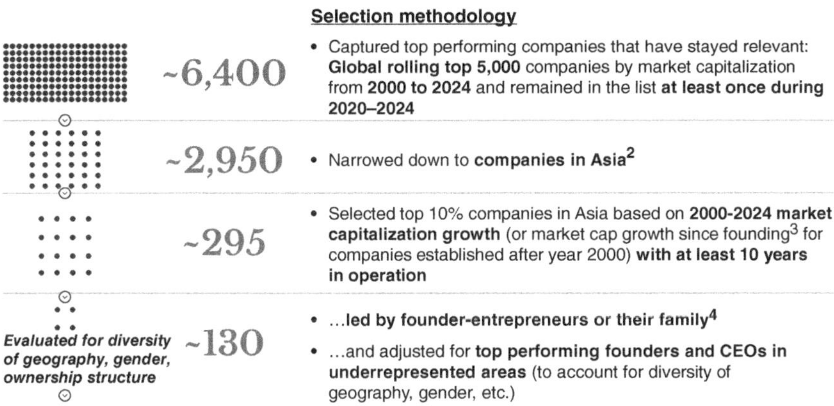

1. Private companies may be underrepresented due to lack of publicly disclosed financial data.
2. Also includes Australia, Azerbaijan, Kazakhstan, New Zealand
3. For companies that have achieved exceptional growth and significant market capitalization addition, but have not yet reached the 20+ years in operation threshold – particularly those in high-growth sectors like internet and platform plays - we have still included this subset provided they have at least 10 years of operating history
4. "Founder-entrepreneur-led" refers to companies in which the original founder or founding family is the largest individual shareholder or retains significant voting influence, including through board or management representation.

How to Read this Book

We have structured this book around behaviors and mindsets. Behaviors are the six key sections that form the majority of the book, and they each examine a particular element of running a business where we have identified common ground in the way founders operate. These include aspects such as attitude to risk, talent, and innovation.

These behaviors are underpinned by 18 governing mindsets, which examine a precise way of thinking founders exhibit. They can be read in any order.

But we also need to ask why founders work this way. So first of all, "Who They Are" looks at the influences that have shaped them: location, philosophy, history, foreign exposure. We also seek to find common ground in their DNA: some consistent personality traits among founders that are useful to understand before we examine their working techniques.

We believe these behaviors are timeless and resilient to disruption. As AI disrupts the world, the founder's essential strengths remain constant: the ability to pivot, navigate uncertainty, embrace contradictions, see opportunity in chaos, and act decisively at speed. In future, humans and machines will work together, the carbon and the silicon in unison. These founder behaviors will matter just as much in the AI era as they did before.

One final point: we use the word *founder* to describe most of our interviewees. Many of the people we have interviewed are second-generation or later members of the family, or in some cases professional CEOs who were part of the founding team promoted from within by founders, but for ease of reading we use the term *founder* to refer to all of these people.

PART I

Who They Are

"If my life story was distillable into an hour, I'd be very disappointed with myself."

—Anand Mahindra

How Founders are Shaped by Their Environment

"Wealth and possessions come and go, but knowledge and wisdom stay with you forever."

—Suphachai Chearavanont, CP Group

If we are to decode the DNA of Asia's leading founder-entrepreneurs, we must first learn something of who they are. We will find, in our diverse list of 30 individuals - among them Chinese, Indians, Japanese, Australians, Hindus, Confucians, Muslims, and Catholics, men and women, crusading new founders and seventh-generation dynasts, wise octogenarians and spritely 40-somethings and every age between - that everyone is, of course, different. But we will also discover some intriguing common ground.

Every founder in our book, covering a 35-year age range, multiple nationalities and different belief systems, is revered in their field. But they are all still people, shaped by the same influences as the rest of us: childhood, religion, teachers, friends, experience.

Every founder we interviewed achieved success by taking a bet on their home country. They used it as a market to grow in and a talent base to recruit from: many Asian nations feature very large populations to sell to and hire within.

What they did next varies from place to place. Some, such as the founders of the banks Bank Central Asia, Kotak Mahindra, and Cathay Financial, stayed chiefly in their home markets of Indonesia, India, and Taiwan, respectively. The domestic opportunity was sufficient to command their full attention.

Some, such as Infosys and Sun Pharma, globalized, making far more revenue from outside their home market than within it – but even then, their founders achieved this by leveraging the talent advantage of India, where they began.

Some, like Michael Kim, founder of MBK Partners in Seoul, saw opportunity in adjacent geographies, expanding into North Asian neighbors, though only where he believed his homegrown team had a competitive advantage.

But in every case, entrepreneurs made their fortunes by hitching their wagons to the countries they came from.

And it is helpful to understand some of the historical and philosophical background that they grew up in because history and philosophy are two of the most powerful influences on the founders in this book.

The Influence of Philosophy

"Confucianism and Daoism are very much in the philosophies of how entrepreneurs manage and lead organizations."

—Jeffrey Li, GL Capital

Just as there is no one Asia, there is also no single unifying philosophy for Asia. Those of India, Japan, and Indonesia are as diverse as those of France, Ethiopia and Mexico. But it is true to say that Asian founders have been influenced by the philosophies distinct to their part of the world.

India and the Arthashastra

Consider, for example, Kautilya's Arthashastra, an ancient Indian Sanskrit text compiled about 2,300 years ago. Kautilya (sometimes known as Chanakya) is considered India's earliest strategist and realist, and the

Arthashastra is thought of as a definitive early treatise on statecraft, politics, and economics.[1]

It's striking how many of Kautilya's teachings find an echo in the practices of modern Indian corporate founders. His philosophy was based on purpose, material well-being, and sustainable prosperity, and he believed that idealism without pragmatism is weakness. This is also mirrored in the view of Reliance Industries Chairman and Managing Director Mukesh Ambani, who believes, "Wealth must have a purpose. It must be used to benefit society." When Ambani champions large-scale infrastructure and access to technology over a long time horizon he reflects the Arthashastra's emphasis on scale, resilience, and strategic dominance rather than just profit.

The Arthashastra also strongly supports meritocracy, incentives for innovation, and the rewarding of competence over lineage. Narayana Murthy, founder of Infosys, expresses a similar mindset when he says, "Progress is possible only when people are free to think, innovate, and take risks." Murthy's own institutional focus on transparency, systems, and professional management resonates with Kautilya's championing of process, accountability, and talent.

Kautilya also had a clear sense of what a leader was: not a monarch by privilege but a servant strategist. The word he used for leader – *rajarsi* – combines the Sanskrit words for *king (raja)* and *sage (rishi)*. He therefore emphasizes the importance of credibility, trust, and reputation, arguing that a ruler or institution with trust can raise resources cheaply but that loss of trust increases cost. This is manifestly true in banking, where a trusted institution has cheaper access to funding. As Uday Kotak, founder of Kotak Mahindra, says, "Capital is scarce. Trust is scarcer. Banks are not about making money in good times; they are about surviving bad times."

Falguni Nayar, Gita, and Freedom

Another highly important Indian scripture is the *Bhagavad Gita*, which synthesizes many strands of Indian religious thought. Falguni Nayar, Founder and CEO of the Indian beauty e-commerce company Nykaa, is one who practices these teachings in business today. "I'm very inspired by a Gita philosophy that says sometimes success happens through you, and not by you," she says. "So you are just an instrument." While she is clearly responsible, with others, for the creation of her company, she finds the idea that its success was meant to happen encouraging. "If you treat it lightly like that, then you're not carrying too much weight of the world on your shoulders," she says. "You can enjoy the journey." Nayar's philosophy on that journey was also shaped by her background. She says she was blessed by an environment where the men in her life – first her father, then her husband, and later her colleagues in banking at Kotak Mahindra – treated her as an equal, enabling her to take risks. "It was quite traditional to say, 'girls don't do this'. But I almost never heard that."

With that freeing attitude, she grew up bold – "I was quite an adventurer at heart, and I never thought of anything as a risk", whether it was trekking in Kashmir on a student exchange program or windsurfing in a lake. That attitude stuck with her, and today when people ask the negative outcome of a risk she takes, "what comes to my mind is more of the thrill of that experience. That thrill was always more on my mind than the likely outcome of a failure." Her philosophical outlook and her life experience have combined to shape her view on risk – and to give her the confidence to start a new business at 50, her age when she founded Nykaa in 2012 after a successful career in investment banking.

China and Confucianism

Confucianism is not so much a religion as a system of thought that dates back at least 2,500 years to ancient China, and is still deeply influential in China, Korea, Japan, and Vietnam, as well as anywhere with a significant Chinese diaspora such as Singapore or Malaysia. Buddhism, which originated in India but became a powerful force in China, Southeast Asia, and Japan, is also highly significant. Also relevant in China is Taoism or Daoism, a philosophical and religious system.

These ideas remain highly important to business leaders today. "Confucian philosophy and Daoism still have an impact on us," says Jeffrey Li, founding partner and CEO of the Chinese healthcare private

Harmony in Family: The Fubon Way

One Chinese idiom close to Daniel Tsai's heart is *xiōng di tong xīn, qi li duan jīn* (**兄弟同心 其力断金**), or "When brothers are of the same mind, their combined strength can cut through metal." One can see why it appeals to Daniel: he and his brother Richard run Fubon Group, the Taiwanese conglomerate that spans financial services, telecommunications, and e-commerce.

Daniel believes the presence of two brothers "makes us different as a family business from others in Taiwan or even Asia. It's very rare for you to see two brothers working so closely."

But it has worked. "If you can work with your brother he is the best partner you can ever have," Daniel says. "You can be so direct and honest. You cannot hide anything from each other." The two consult in making decisions, knowing one another's weaknesses and strengths. "It's a very unusual personal journey."

equity firm GL Capital. "These things are very much in the philosophies of how entrepreneurs manage and lead organizations."

In its principle of "governing the world" *yǐ rú zhì shì* (以儒治世), there is a relevance for business: Confucianism reminds leaders that companies are communities, not machines, and that the leader's role in such a world is to uphold righteousness over expedience, trust over control, and benevolence over fear. Companies have an important role to play within a broader community-first world order. A key Confucian value is harmony, illustrated in the two boxes in this chapter, "Harmony in Family: The Fubon Way" and "How Philosophy Influences Leadership: An Example."

The more interesting question is *how* it has worked, and perhaps here Confucian values of harmony are relevant. The two brothers have accepted the compromises that are needed in joint decision-making, having decided that the outcome is well worth the effort. But this would not be possible without a philosophical disposition toward equanimity. "If the family does not have harmony, the business cannot have harmony, and society cannot have harmony," he says. "It starts with immediate family members. Living under the same roof is tough enough. Working under the same roof is tougher still. My brother and I have found a way."

Daniel finds something distinctive to Asian values in the way his relationship works. "This is something the Asian business family really is: we come back to our roots, to our culture, to our heritage, and find the right values for ourselves, our families and society," he says.

How Philosophy Influences Leadership: An Example

Harmony, which emphasizes a delicate balance between extremes, is implicit in Confucianism. We see an example of this harmony in lived practice in Seok Cho, the Vice Chairman of HD Korea Shipbuilding and Offshore Engineering.[2]

Cho is unusual in this book in that he does not consider himself a classic entrepreneur. In fact, he has the humility to look up to them – "they possess a duality: they have unique ideas and an exceptional ability to align with global trends while pursuing profit" – but he doesn't think that's what he's there for.

Instead Cho describes himself as being a harmonizer – by which he means something different from facilitation, but instead one who focuses

Suphachai Chearavanont, Senior Vice Chairman of the Thailand-based conglomerate CP Group (see "The Culture That Shaped CP Group"), expresses a corporate outlook that closely reflects this way of thinking. "CP is about focusing on the greater good – the 'three benefits' philosophy," he says. This means that "if you invest and operate in a country, the country must benefit and the people of the country must benefit. And then the company can benefit."

Another important ideal is the Daoist idea of cultivating the self *yǐ dào zhì shēn* (以道治身), and in particular the idea of *wú wéi ér zhì* on balance. It's a mindset he developed in resolving a dispute between the production and sales teams in the power equipment business shortly after he joined the company.

In a business context, he sees balance as meaning no single area becomes overly dominant. It links with tolerance and a willingness to hear differing opinions and unconventional perspectives.

"Balance is an abstract concept. What's important, I think, is making the effort." Achieving perfect harmony or balance is unrealistic. "But recognizing its importance and constantly striving for it is what matters."

(无为而治), or non-forcing and "no rule rules." This idea suggest the highest form of management uses minimal rules and structures. Leaders should move with the flow of change rather than against it. Most obviously, we see this in modern business in an ability to perceive what the market wants – or, better still, is going to want next – and to adapt to that changing need in order to be successful. Daoist self-cultivation also speaks to calmness amid volatility – just as many of our entrepreneurs learned to adapt to changing forces under stress and at speed during the COVID-19 pandemic.

The Culture That Shaped CP Group

Charoen Pokphand Group, or CP, is Thailand's largest private company, a multi-business conglomerate founded in 1921 and owned by the Chearavanont family. Suphachai, the Senior Vice Chairman, is the third generation of the dynasty.

Suphachai notes the impact of both Chinese and Thai culture, religion, and attitudes in his own upbringing. He was raised with many brothers, sisters, and cousins, learning from it a sense of community and respect towards elders.

One of the main values he learned in childhood is expressed in Thai as Katanyu (กตัญญู) (*Kataññū),* which means gratitude toward parents or anyone who supported him in childhood. "These values – gratitude, family responsibility – combined with our great religion and culture to shape me," he says. "We are products of that tradition and leadership, rooted in the national institutions and cultural traditions that have shaped Thai leadership values."

We see this sense of humility in a policy CP Group holds toward family members, implemented by Suphachai's father and uncle: that no family members should join established businesses. Instead, they should start something new. "That way, we learn and prove we can create

The Art of War

The Art of War was written about 2,500 years ago by the Chinese military strategist Sun Tzu. While this is, in its origins, a military text, it has become increasingly popular to find in it lessons for business – an appreciation that has spread far beyond China (the Gordon Gekko character references it frequently in *Wall Street*, which came out in 1987).

value." The feeling is that established businesses are already well run with robust systems and strong professionals; a family member moving into such a business would simply be gaining from the work of others, and would learn little. "Joining something at its starting point gives you a perspective on building from zero," says Suphachai, whose own path took him through a fledgling telecom business.

He was also shaped by the influence of his mother, who instilled in him two things: the importance of knowledge and the need for courage. "The only treasure you truly have is your knowledge," she told him. "Never think you can depend on your father's wealth or possessions – those can come and go. But knowledge and wisdom stay with you forever." She also explained the need for dignity in self-preservation. "She taught us to be fighters," he says. "Not to fight people unnecessarily, but to have courage and stand up for what we believe in."

This was useful as Suphachai attended seven schools around the world as the family moved. "You had to adapt yourself a lot because you don't exactly belong anywhere," he says. "But all these struggles, including moving to the US, taught me that I've been through many cultural changes." Today he adapts this into staff development, telling his human resources team: "Rotate, rotate, rotate the people."

There are many Sun Tzu aphorisms favored in business in China and, increasingly, elsewhere. They are, of course, applied metaphorically in business rather than as a practical guide for adversarial or ruthless conduct, but in that context the lessons are potent. "Every battle is won before it is fought" (sometimes expressed as "Win before you fight") speaks to preparation and planning. "If you know the enemy and know yourself, you need not fear the result of a hundred battles" (sometimes "know yourself and your opponent") is fundamentally about marketplace and competitive analysis. "Opportunities multiply as they are seized" mirrors the agility and ability to pivot of modern founder-entrepreneurs.

Sun Tzu also instructed leaders to lead by example, not by force. "Lead with the right people – leadership and talent decide outcomes," he wrote, and "leverage momentum and timing – speed, flexibility, and situation control."

Japanese Belief Systems

Japanese founders often bring a philosophical element to their work, reflecting their belief system going back to childhood. Buddhism and Confucianism are still highly relevant here, but so is another more distinct Japanese ideology.

The Shu Ha Ri (守破離 (しゅはり)) philosophy – keeping, breaking, and separating – raises some interesting contradictions for founders. Shu speaks to respect for hierarchy and collective harmony, Ha to challenging it. It is in the Ha part of Japanese philosophy that we find the most classic entrepreneurial spirit: the need to challenge, to iterate. The skill of Japanese founders is to break the rules without appearing disrespectful to tradition.

President and CEO Takahisa Takahara cites this philosophy explicitly in defining his own management style at Unicharm, the Japanese manufacturer of personal care and hygiene products, founded by his father in Tokyo in 1961. Takahara practices Shu through the mastery of preserving the fundamentals, Ha through innovation and breaking norms, and Ri through the creation of something new by doing so.

The Influence of History

> *"We come back to our roots, to our culture, to our heritage."*
> —Daniel Tsai, Fubon Group

The founder-entrepreneurs profiled in this book cover an age range of several decades, but all of them grew up at extremely interesting times for their country. We don't have space to examine the recent history of every Asian country, but again it is instructive to look at what has happened in the two biggest, India and China.

Post-Colonial India

The founders of India's most remarkable family businesses – names such as the Birlas and Tatas – were in a way a response to a pre-independence era in which India's centuries of trade traditions were under bureaucratic control. When the British left and India became independent in 1947, those mercantile ways of life were twinned with a zest to unleash the newly independent country in the way it built its companies, trade, and government.

When third-generation leader Anand Mahindra steered the automobile manufacturing company Mahindra & Mahindra from its domestic origins to being a true multinational in the early 2000s, he felt that defining the company as global had some symbolism in light of the country's own evolution. "We wanted to get out of our colonial complexes and the lack of self-confidence, an inferiority complex that was a legacy of colonialism," he says. "We needed to believe in ourselves."

Many of our interviewees – such as Infosys Founder Narayana Murthy, HDFC Bank Founder Aditya Puri, and Anand Mahindra – were born in the decade after World War II and gained their social and business awareness during the post-independence socialist Nehru era, which created its own momentum.

In 1975 Murthy, who would go on to found transformational Indian multinational technology company Infosys six years later, coined a new term, *compassionate capitalism*, to combine the best elements of capitalism he had been exposed to while working in Europe with the Nehru ideology he had grown up with as the son of a teacher in a lower-middle-class family.

Also, many of the country's future leaders grew up in quite modest circumstances during the Nehru era, in ways that would shape them in later life. Uday Kotak was raised in a joint family with 63 family members in one home, sharing one kitchen. It sounds unworkable; the family made it work. He never forgot it. When it came to building the bank Kotak Mahindra, which he launched in 1985, he understood from that time that people could find ways to work together. "It created significant bonding," he says.

Aditya Puri grew up with a sense of humility from childhood. His father was a Wing Commander in the Indian Air Force – so not a poor background by any means, but a frugal one with a certain moral standard forever present. "You were used to sharing a coke, you were used to wearing Bata shoes.[1] You were value-for-money conscious, bloody hard-working, and you had good ethics."

Those values were handy when Puri came back to India to launch HDFC Bank in 1994, having already made a name for himself at Citi in Malaysia, where he earned considerably more money than he would do in the early days setting up the new bank in India.

When he started out in Mumbai's Sandoz House, which was being renovated at the time, "I was sitting in an office with a broken chair," he recalls. Recognizing that he wasn't going to be able to make key hires from American banks with that sort of a corporate backdrop, he was therefore forced to focus very clearly on his story and his intentions, as that was the only way he would get good people to join him.

These small beginnings did not stop HDFC Bank from becoming one of India's preeminent banks, and perhaps in some sense they contributed to what it became. Puri never lost his sense that one could learn from grassroots engagement with the customer, and humility enabled him to listen to them.

In all these cases, the modesty of their beginnings influenced the way they viewed the world and what they wanted to do with it. Kotak took the spirit of community and tolerance into shaping his team to build a bank. Murthy's almost obsessive desire for respect came from his upbringing. Puri's values were highly relevant when he set a clearly stated principle that HDFC Bank would go nowhere near bribery or corruption, partly out of a useful ignorance. "With an Armed Forces background you grew up in a particular way," he says. "We didn't know what a bribe was. We wouldn't know how to do it."

Indian Liberalization

From 1991, liberalization dismantled earlier barriers and unleashed India's private sector. Those who had seen it coming thrived. Kotak Mahindra had been finding its feet for six years by 1991, Sun Pharma for eight, and both went from strength to strength when liberalization arrived. Aditya Puri founded HDFC Bank three years later and accelerated with the new opportunity.

Today those names – and older Indian groups such as Biocon, Bajaj, Reliance, Mahindra & Mahindra, and Infosys[2] – thrive in the world's fifth-largest economy, worth US$4.1 trillion in 2024 and growing at 6–7% annually, the fastest and most consistent among major economies. It is a country of 900 million internet users and 10 billion digital transactions a month.[3]

Indians have brought to the business world an ambition fueled by having something to prove, and it was liberalization that gave them the opportunity to prove it. Pent-up ability has proven an extremely potent force.

China: Moving Forward

China's social and commercial traditions go back more than two millennia, much of them structured on a centralized state order and the ideas of collective harmony and meritocracy found in Confucianism. Discipline and mastery, attributes of the imperial civil service system going back centuries, are still important corporate and educational values in China today.

Where India was under British control, China had its own challenges starting with the Opium Wars in the 1800s; indeed, there is an era of history from the start of the First Opium War in 1839 to the end of World War II in 1945 that is known in China as the *Century of Humiliation (bǎi nián guó chǐ)* (百年国耻).

Just like in India, the late 1940s[4] prompted a desire for a form of national restoration, but it was not a smooth journey.

Many Chinese founders grew up with the backdrop of the Cultural Revolution and were deeply affected by the experience, with a strong desire to do something better for the country. Jeffrey Li at GL Capital (see Jeffrey

Jeffrey Li and the Fortune of Timing

Jeffrey Li, the founder of GL Capital, was born in 1963 and experienced the Cultural Revolution during childhood.

"We benefited from being the first generation to be able to have a college education again. And then, we were the first generation to go abroad." He was among the first to go to the United States in the wave of young Chinese people who discovered the world as students. "When I went to the US to study for my master's degree, it was eye-opening." He started reading *Business Week* and *Fortune*, and began trading the stock market to make some money, becoming an avid disciple of articles by Warren Buffett and his investment techniques.

He got lucky again when he came back to China as Deng Xiaoping began to open and reform the economy. And so he was able to make the best of the good fortune of his timing and exposure.

"I think our generation of entrepreneurs from China really have the benefit of the best of both worlds," he says. From the West, they learned business systems, talent organization, strategy, marketing, operations, and investments. "We were able to go there and get exposed to all of that and then say, 'wow, these things are really good.'" And then they came home and had the benefits of rich Chinese culture, with its thousands of years of Confucian and Daoist philosophy. "These things are very much in the philosophies of how entrepreneurs manage and lead organizations."

"If you put them together, that's the best way."

Li and the "Fortune of Timing") was someone who felt this way. "In the 1980s, China was still very early in its development," he says. "The country was largely closed and much poorer than it is today." That pushed him forward to improve.

The sense that hard work could be a ticket out of a bad situation is also an enormously forceful impetus. "That's how we Chinese succeeded," says Li. "We just work harder than other people." He applies it now as a mantra at GL Capital. "How can we be a successful firm if we do not work at least as hard as all the other players, and hopefully harder? There's no replacement for that."

The Power of International Exposure

"That experience changed my life."

—Jane Sun, Trip.com Group

It is striking how many of our interviewees were profoundly influenced by exposure to another culture while young. Jeffrey Li was transformed by US education, as were Trip.com Group's Jane Sun and Foxconn's Sidney Lu (see "Jane Sun and Giving Back" and "Sidney Lu: Eastern Discipline, Western Mindset, and a Devoted Mother"), while Narayana Murthy's ideas of compassionate capitalism stemmed from his time in Paris. Anand Mahindra took time to study filmmaking at Harvard College in order to prove that he was something more than an anointed successor at an established dynasty. Akio Nitori was heavily influenced by the United States, and sought to bring the attributes he found there back to Japan. Jaime Augusto Zóbel de Ayala, seventh-generation leader of the Ayala Group, studied in the United Kingdom and the United States and brought insights back to the Philippines.

Jane Sun and Giving Back

Jane Sun was offered an opportunity to study in the United States during her university years. But at that time, she struggled financially: her parents, both chemistry engineers, didn't earn nearly enough to support the costs of studying in America.

So she worked. Alongside her studies she put in almost 40 hours a week making US$3 an hour. It was enough to cover her tuition, but not her food. And it limited her to three or four hours of sleep per night – a habit she can still tolerate today.

Seeing her situation, her professor's family took her in. "They treated me as their own daughter," she says now. Raised with Confucian values of looking after parents, she told them that she hoped to be able to do the same for them; they explained that it wasn't necessary, and that Western values tended in the other direction, to support the child. So she found another way to express her gratitude.

Many years later in 2016, when she became CEO of the global travel services provider Trip.com Group, she had succeeded sufficiently in business to establish a scholarship, which she named after the professor's family. She also named her daughter after his wife. They still meet frequently; Sun flew to celebrate the wife's 90th, 91st, and 92nd birthdays with her. "She is like my mother to me and we celebrate whenever I go to the states to have a business meeting."

"That experience changed my life."

Exposure to foreign enterprises has also been deeply important to the development of many Asian founder-entrepreneurs. Uday Kotak, founder of Kotak Mahindra, learned how to build a world-class institution from his early partnerships with Goldman Sachs and Ford Credit. Joseph Tsai, Vice Chairman at Cathay Financial and the third generation of his family to serve the bank, learned a great deal about culture from having worked at Goldman Sachs and US law firms. Much of the cultural change he enacted at Cathay comes from what he had learned there – such as the Western practice of speaking up, no matter what rank one holds in the organization. At Cathay he had to work out how to empower people to express an opinion, which was new to them. "Maybe I'm a little more Western in my thinking," he says today.

Saehong Hur, Board Chair and CEO at South Korean energy and chemical company GS Caltex, spent time in a manufacturing company in Japan, then later IBM and Chevron; it took him 18 years to find his way back to Seoul and he brought a great deal of accumulated learning with him when he did. "Such diverse working experiences in different countries really helped me develop situational leadership and a flexibility for different market situations and cultures," he says.

Korean has its own equivalent of the English idiom about imagining being in another person's shoes; Hur cites it often. It has led him to a principle of what he calls "we-dership" which refers to "leadership we build together." "It means we lead together not only at the top but also at the bottom of the field," he explains, and it comes partly from his exposure to a range of cultures and the sense that one can learn new things from anyone. "Meeting different types of people helps me develop a new intuition for the future," he says.

But the importance of all this exposure is that those who would go on to be founders did not just sit wide-eyed and impressed at what they saw, but thought hard about how to ally their learnings with their own local

Sidney Lu: Eastern Discipline, Western Mindset, and a Devoted Mother

Sidney Lu was the founding CEO and Chairman of Foxconn Interconnect Technology, the subsidiary of Hon Hai Precision,[2] which specializes in the development of cables and connectors. He is a leader who has combined Eastern philosophy and discipline with a Western mindset and education.

His time at the University of Illinois at Urbana-Champaign helped him to combine the Confucian and Daoist influences of his childhood with something different. "That Western education gave me self-confidence and self-love," he says. "You've got to love yourself because if you don't, don't expect anyone else to love you. We all have our own faults, don't beat yourself up."

This was a lesson Sidney had started to learn at 14, when he took his high school entrance exam alongside his twin brother, Christopher. Sidney missed out on his first-choice school; his brother was selected. "It was the first time I lost out. It was a big setback and shock to me at the time," he says.

cultures and blend the two together. Michael Kim, for example, twinned his background with the cultural lessons of the West to develop what he saw as a contribution to a distinct Asian form of capitalism when he set up MBK Partners in Seoul.

An interesting aside to this is that Asia has its own patterns of influence and migration within the continent: many of the world's most important trading routes are intra-Asian so it's natural that people and ideas flow with them.

A fascinating example of this is CP Group, which has a century of history in Thailand[1] but traces its origins to two Chinese immigrant brothers, Chia Ek Chor and Chia Jin Hyang, from Swatow in Guangdong. CP has

In Asia, moments like this can be debilitating; children tend not to be quick to move on from failure with confidence, and parents may be unwilling to let them do so. But Sidney's mother was keen to teach him something. "I remember my mother, as I was wallowing in self-pity, said, 'What are you going to do about it? Move on. It's done.'" His brother had worked harder, she said, so take the lesson and get over it.

"It's the first lesson I learned," he says. "Take ownership, take accountability, don't wallow in past failures. What's important is what's ahead." A hugely influential figure in the boys' lives, she would go on to follow them to Illinois, renting an apartment near their dorm, cooking for them and supporting them before spending her spare time learning English in a local community college.

The combination of an Asian upbringing, supportive mother, and Western education proved a powerful cocktail for Lu. Eastern values taught him discipline, humility, hard work, and respect; Western values taught him self-belief and a willingness to accept failure. All these attributes can be found in Foxconn's guiding principles today, which include integrity, diligence, and collaboration.[3]

retained a strong connection with China, and was the first foreign company registered in the special economic zone of Shenzhen after China began to open in 1978 (its corporate registration number there, 0001, is a source of some pride today). Today CP has 200 business subsidiaries in mainland China.

This migratory spirit is important to the company's soul, says Suphachai Chearavanont. "I say *entrepreneur* is a good word for a well-rounded spirit of explorers," he says. Why, he asks, are many countries so dynamic and strong culturally? "Because of migrants. Even now, in the second or third generation, that migrant spirit still supports the economy and culture."

Many founders were shaped by their experience overseas while young. They took the ideas they found in the West and applied them in their own lives as they set about building new enterprises in Asia. Many have continued to learn from other markets throughout their careers, adapting what they see to their home – and often improving on it.

Catalysts for Restoring Asia's Preeminence

What does this all mean today? From 2,000 years ago until the early 19th century, Asia produced roughly two-thirds of global gross domestic product,[1] according to Angus Maddison's *Contours of the World Economy 1–2030*AD. Taking a view over truly long-term history tells us that the modern era's Western dominance is a historically brief interlude rather than the long-run norm. Whether we believe Maddison's analysis or not, most of our founders have a strong belief in the spirit of that study.

All indications are that Asian dominance of the world economy is returning, and all of these influences of old and recent history – philosophy, colonialism, foreign influence, independence, hope – shape leading founders today. Key business leaders have emerged who seek to challenge status quo. By learning from the past, embracing belief systems that were once preeminent, and absorbing the lessons of foreign exposure, these people are releasing their ability.

Figure P.1 Two Thousand Years of Economic History

Source: "Statistics on World Population, GDP, and per capita GDP, 1-2008 CE". Angus Maddison, University of Groningen.

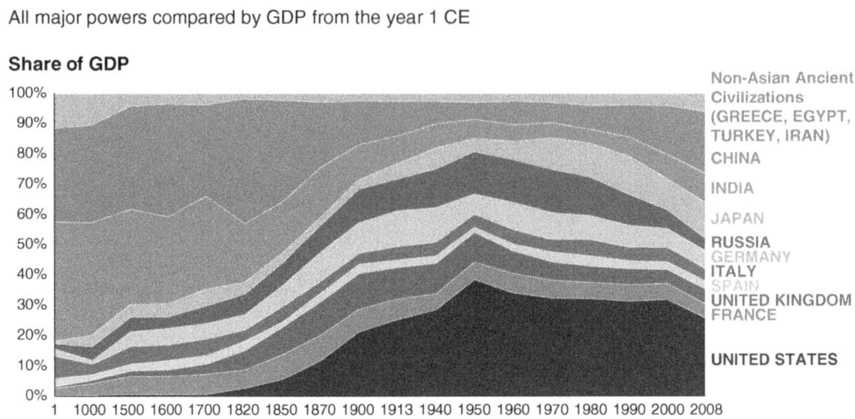

The last half century in Asia hasn't just fostered a workforce to build new things and a consumer base to buy them. It has also spurred innovation in its own right because of the surroundings within which Asian founders have grown up and been shaped. Born to adapt, they are acclimatized to volatility, used to spotting opportunity windows that might last only months, and embrace a regional or national psyche oriented toward acceleration.

This complex context has created an innate desire to reclaim what's been lost, and to succeed on a different scale and with a more brazen boldness than would otherwise have been the case. The sense of entering and shaping a new era has fostered a time horizon that spans not just decades but generations. The founders in this book have aimed remarkably high, and as each of them has succeeded on a national scale they have created an aggregate that has helped bring the Asian age back once again.

The Traits That Bind Founders

"Is there someone out there with a different perspective?"
—Seok Cho, HD Hyundai Electric

Our founders are bonded by some consistent traits. They include speed of decision-making, a desire for continuous learning, and an understanding of the importance of relationships. Founders possess an immense personal energy that manifests itself in a dissatisfaction at the status quo and a desire to do more. Most consider their work their life, and their life their work.

And they all show a rare ability that recalls F. Scott Fitzgerald's claim that the hallmark of first-rate intelligence is "the ability to hold two opposed ideas in the mind at the same time and still retain the ability to function."[1]

Comfortable with Contradictions

Founders are exceptional at doing what Fitzgerald described. Their work is full of contradictions, but they embrace them. For example, they want to manage risk to ensure the long-term viability of their business and its performance for stakeholders, but they also understand the occasional need for definitive and transformational big bets. They want to grow big, to scale their successes, but they also want to preserve the culture that shaped the company when it was small.

The outlier founders we profile in this book have an innate ability to manage these conundrums, aided perhaps by a length of time frame that a professional CEO cannot count on since professionals are often hired for as little as three to five years. It doesn't appear to bother them that their days are filled with the management of contradictions at every level. They vary from the development of talent (they seek the extraordinary from their people, yet in Asia's talent-scarce environment they must coax it from those who, when hired, are not yet extraordinary) to their whole sense of purpose (in setting out with a mission quite beyond the simple pursuit of profit, they have made significant wealth).

One reason they are so good at this is because of a skill in understanding where they should best spend their time to add value. They know which decisions are critical, and that only they can make; they know what to trust others to lead. They are purposeful in their allocation of time, and they direct that time toward the things that only they can do. Seeing their role on a multi-decade canvas – in fact a multigenerational one, when their work will conclude with handing the enterprise over to others – they are able to step back and see where their time is required in the pursuit of very long-term objectives.

Also, what seems like a contradiction to many may not feel that way to a founder, as they have the skill to integrate differing ideas rather than to see them as in opposition. They do not see things as housed in tight compartments, and consequently are skilled in balancing them.

Decisive

Founders know how to make a decision with speed. They may have different techniques for reaching that decision, from individual gut to wide consultation, but they get there at speed. Then they execute with the self-confidence that comes with being an owner.

Some design for speed. Michael Kim founded MBK Partners in the knowledge that it would be important to be nimble, and that this could only be achieved by making big decisions quickly. From his time at global firms like Goldman Sachs where it could take three or four days to set up an investment committee call with decision-makers, he knew speed could be an advantage.

"We decided on day one when we had a decision to make as a committee, we would drop everything else," he says. Whole-team calls are scheduled on an hour's notice, and senior people are expected to attend no matter what else is happening. That enables them to submit unconditional bids before the competition.

"We had a commitment to speed. When it came to decision-making no one was going to be faster or more nimble than us," he says. He recalls a Chinese saying *sù zhàn sù jué* (速战速决) (and its Korean equivalent *Sokjeon Sokgyeol*), which means "fast battle, fast decision." "It's basically blitzkrieg, and it's a huge competitive advantage."

This philosophy has given Kim and his team an edge. "For us, the combination of nimble decision-making combined with a long-term horizon was the winning formula."

The method of achieving a decision varies, however, and is not always just about gut instinct. Narayana Murthy at Infosys places hard numbers at the heart of his decision-making. "Most decisions of mine come from data and analysis using mathematical and statistical models," he says. "I do not know what intuition is and I have never used it. I do not understand what I cannot measure."

A long-standing fan of data analysis well before it became fashionable, during his time leading Infosys Murthy computed as precisely as he could the expected value of the outcome of a decision. "If that value was acceptable to us we would go ahead with our decision." There's a place for judgment, he believes, but it follows rather than precedes the data. "It is a good idea to superimpose the experience and the judgement of senior leaders on what data says."

Some seek consultation. Seok Cho at HD Hyundai Electric forces himself not to settle for a single perspective. "If someone presents a compelling argument, I often ask myself, 'What if they're wrong? Is there someone out there with a different perspective?'" Actively seeking out opposing viewpoints gives him the context to make balanced decisions.

Continuous Learner

A common characteristic among founder-entrepreneurs is curiosity. They never stop learning – and never stop wanting to do so. This curiosity becomes a business differentiator, as being the fastest learner helps a founder and their institution to be agile. They understand that they are only as good as what they know.

"I've always believed you learn from everybody you interact with if you have an open mind," says Sanjiv Bajaj, Chairman and Managing Director of the Pune-headquartered financial services company Bajaj Finserv and the fourth generation of the Bajaj family to serve the company since the Bajaj

Group's foundation in 1926. "That's why to me, listening before talking is always important."

It is a common belief among founders that they can learn from other people – and it doesn't matter if they're junior members of their own organization, people in entirely different industries, or competitors.

Takahara at Unicharm has a phrase for his approach to learning from others: "Enriching your own drawer." The metaphorical drawer in question is filled with business proposals and organizational frameworks he will present at the right time; to keep that drawer full, he seeks new insights from external connections, attending industry meetings and learning about other companies' governance practices. He speaks of "external stimuli circulating internally" as a major motivational factor.

Curiosity is potent not only as a mechanism to learn but also to keep oneself motivated and always seeking new horizons. For Anand Mahindra, "that's what kept my personal energies up: it was curiosity." Mahindra studied film before moving into business, and wanted to retain some sense of creativity in his work; curiosity was the prism through which he was able to see that creativity.

Jane Sun at Trip.com Group believes part of the whole appeal for the travel industry within which she has made her name is the ability to learn. "One of the reasons travel is so good is that when you're in a strange place, if you learn about language, culture, and history, that keeps your mind stimulated."

It takes a certain humility to accept that there are things one does not know and can learn from others. One would not ordinarily associate these strong-minded and driven business leaders with humility, but it is a vital part of how they absorb information. Many founders speak of their belief that they can learn something new from anyone they speak to, both within and outside their organization.

Relationship Builder

Founder-entrepreneurs tend to be highly relationship-oriented people. They sense and build relationship networks and understand this to be fundamental to their growth, both individually and in the companies they build.

They build connected webs of people, recognizing that the interactions between them are useful. More than networking, this is about the depth and breadth of the connections they create.

Many founders build relationships the same way all of us do: by getting out there and pressing the flesh. "One of my strengths is I'm a great networker," says Kiran Mazumdar-Shaw, who founded the Indian biotech Biocon in her Bengaluru garage in 1978. "I'm very interested in networking with scientists."

She attends conferences, serving on the boards of MIT and Memorial Sloan Kettering, all of which provide her with plentiful sources of information, information technology, and sometimes talent. It's instructive that she has filled her board with connected experts. Charles Cooney, who was Head of the Biochemical Engineering Department at MIT, was on her first board; others who have served include biotech entrepreneur Bala Manian.

Sanjiv Bajaj believes strongly in the importance of networking within his own organization. He surrounds himself with people (people, he jokes, who are smarter than he is): members of Bajaj Group boards, key CEOs, people one or two levels down the corporate hierarchy with a specialist knowledge, and technology officers from Bajaj Finserv's nine operating companies. Over a cup of coffee or a beer he informally engages to understand their priorities, challenges, and opportunities.

For Bajaj, the importance of an internal network of relationships is as key as an external one. For all our entrepreneurs, investment in relationships both internally and externally helps them to drive their business.

Boundless Energy

Asian founders tend to be bonded by a sense of insatiable appetite and restless energy. They are never satisfied with themselves and always want more. Their intense drive for constant improvement and reinvention helps to explain why some of them stay so long in their position, and think on such distant time frames.

Many of these attitudes stem from the intense hard graft of early days. Akio Nitori, who founded the Japanese furniture and home furnishings company Nitori Holdings in 1967, says at 81 (at the time of writing) he has "almost no rest" beyond playing golf and training daily in the company gym ("Maintaining muscle keeps the mind sharp."). Perhaps his energy recalls the early days of trying to find suppliers, long before Nitori took over the entirety of its own value chain including manufacturing. Back then, he remembers going to Taiwan and scouring phone books to find suppliers himself, with local guides, visiting each one, 10 or more places a day, maybe 70 per week. Only 10% were promising.

He says maybe one factory in a hundred would succeed. But it had to be done.

"That was the repetition, the accumulation," he says. "That's how I could offer unknown, inexpensive products to Japan."

Sidney Lu of Foxconn recalls working a 36-hour shift on a Hon Hai factory floor to try to diagnose and fix a problem, not a surprise to those who know him as a regular half-marathon runner who is always first to work each day even at the age of 67. That day on the factory floor he told Foxconn Founder Terry Gou why he was going to work on the midnight shift despite having arrived from overseas the same day: "This is an emergency, there's no time to waste. Midnight is the best time for me to go on the floor and observe what is happening without the managers. It's the best way to understand what the problem is."

Perhaps his attitude stemmed from the lessons he learned missing out on his preferred high school all those years earlier, when his brother was selected instead. "While you were sleeping, he was still studying," his mother said to him then about his brother. "It's not just about intelligence. Someone worked much harder than you did."

That work ethic has informed his whole attitude to leadership. "You cannot be ingenuine. You cannot be a fake. Do the hard work and roll up your sleeves." But he finds it easier to do so because of a common attribute among founders: this is his passion. "I genuinely enjoy my work. I really love what I do."

"That's what gets you out of bed early and makes you jump into work," he says. "You wake up and think, 'This is going to be fun.'"

That word appears with surprising frequency among our interviewees. "I enjoy what I'm doing," says Itaru Tanimura, who founded the healthcare technology company M3 in Tokyo in 2000. "It's fun, and I'm grateful to have people who support me." Mikhail Lomtadze, founder of Kazakhstan super-app Kaspi, doesn't even think of what he does as work. "I really have a lot of fun," he says.

Founders tend not to have a problem with how hard they work. For these people, work is life; it's not about balance between the two as they are one and the same.

So while Jeffrey Li at GL Capital says, "At the end of the day, if you don't have happiness, everything else is meaningless," he's also clear that his company is a part of that happiness. "Everything I do, including GL, is in the equation of my happiness of life," he says. "We look at GL as a journey of life for everyone."

"Don't look at your job separately from your life."

Their energy is also driven by a sense of intensity, even obsession. Several elements feed into this intensity: a fear of not succeeding in what they see as their mission, and a sense of responsibility given the power they have, and the wider impact beyond themselves of the choices they make.

"To want to be an entrepreneur – it had become a life's mission," says Nykaa Founder Falguni Nayar. Having achieved that mission, she derives great joy from it. "Every day I am gifted more hours to grow my knowledge of the business." Nayar does not just love her work, but sees it as a privilege to do what she does: a powerful source of boundless energy.

It should be noted that this work-life integration is not an option for many women. And it certainly wasn't in the era when most of the founders in this book were getting started, which may help to explain why there are so few female founders at the top. It is also not a worldview that will resonate with everyone, regardless of gender. The point is simply this: the founders we interviewed chose to invest their time in what gave them energy and purpose, and in doing so, found the delineation between work and life blurred.

We have learned about how founders are shaped by philosophy, history, and foreign exposure, and the traits they have in common. That tells us who they are.

Now it's time to see how all those traits and influences manifest themselves in how they operate. In the next sections of the book we will delve into founders' six behaviors – across mission, strategy, risk, innovation, talent, and scaling – and their 18 governing mindsets. This provides an insight into their operating practices and offers a glimpse into what makes them so uniquely successful.

There is a distinction between these two fundamentals – who they are and how they operate – and only by examining both can we decode the DNA of founders, and come to understand how and why they create such outsize value.

PART II

How They Operate

"If you're not doing something that's never been done before, what's the point?"

—Mukesh Ambani, Reliance Industries

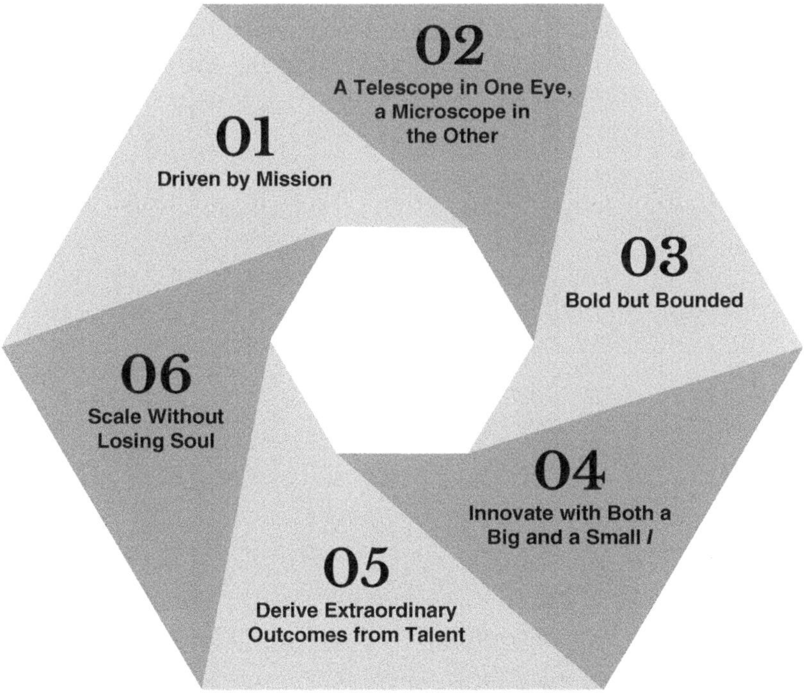

Driven by Mission

"If you do not have a purpose it will not work."
—Mukesh Ambani, Reliance Industries

Governing Mindsets

- **I am a pioneer.**
- **I have insatiable hunger to build.**
- **I succeed if my nation and community succeed.**

"If you want to start a business to be a billionaire, you are an idiot. You will never get there. If you want to start a business to impact a billion people, then you have a good chance of success, and as a by-product you will make money."

Mukesh Ambani, the Chairman and Managing Director of Reliance Industries, is recalling the advice of his father, Dhirubhai, who founded the company in 1957. The lesson has stood the test of time: in ignoring the allure of quick profit and thinking instead of service of a vast market to the betterment of the country, both father and son did a lot more than become billionaires. They built India's largest company[1] and biggest exporter, with a leadership position across a host of sectors from textiles to telecommunications, energy to retail.

And in so doing, they changed India itself, as an employer, as an innovator, and as a force in the world. The business grew with India, bonded and rising together.

"The North Star has always remained: if you do not have a purpose it will not work," Mukesh says. "And purpose has to be impact-led."

Dhirubhai founded Reliance a decade after India's independence, and in his ambition was something bigger than corporate success: it was proving a point, that India could succeed post-colonialism and had great things to offer to the world. Dhirubhai felt, and Mukesh continues to believe, that business is about a societal and nation-shaping purpose as much as it is about profit, and that one will enable the other. This manifests itself over extremely long, multigenerational time frames, and builds for society along the way.

One of the most essential things to understand when we ask what sets Asian founders apart is this sense of a grand intent bigger than business. All through this book we will find evidence of the same determined, society-shaping intent fueled by a deep personal conviction, whether in India, China, Japan, or Southeast Asia. Many founders state their ambitions in a national and social context, with something of a missionary zeal: a feeling that their task in life is to do something remarkable, to create something new and transformational, over a time horizon that can span generations.

This isn't altruism, and we should not be so naive to confuse it as such. It's also smart. If a guiding North Star involves the creation of a new market or the improvement of a country's position in a global industry, or increases wealth to a population who then have greater capacity to spend, that's clearly very good for business. But it requires an extremely long-term lens, as befits founders who behave as if they will be around forever. It's a common characteristic that founders operate as if they are never going to die, and this mindset lends itself extremely well to mission at scale.

Chapter One

I Am a Pioneer

"I have always tried to challenge the status quo."
—Kiran Mazumdar-Shaw, Biocon

It is not enough to describe Asia's founder-entrepreneurs as ambitious. That is to understate the scale of what they wish to achieve. They are people of deep personal conviction who see themselves as missionaries and whose task in life is transformation: to be first, to drive change, to create something valuable and new. They are pioneers.

This plays out in characteristics distinct to founders. One is an outsized time horizon, which gives them the room to build. Another is the importance of being first to some landmark, whether it be a new technology, product, or market. A third is to believe that what they do strengthens their nation and society.

Aiming Long – Very Long

It is very common for founder-entrepreneurs to state their missions in the context of multi-decade development, and this is one of the biggest differentiators between the founder-entrepreneurs who populate this book and professional CEOs.

A professional CEO, who typically has a finite horizon at a company, will align with an existing purpose and the agenda to effect it, but it's not entirely what they're hired for: that's growth, profitability, governance, institutional processes, and strategic direction. Founders seek something

Mission and Service

Akio Nitori, founder of furniture retailer Nitori in Japan, talks about keeping mission at the center of management; in Japanese, he says, that means serving people and society. Deeply impressed by time he spent in the United States at 27, he wanted to bring Japanese living conditions to the same level. "Seeing US models helped me reverse-engineer how to enrich Japanese living," he says. "I calculated what was needed to achieve a richer lifestyle in Japan, learning from US chain stores." He concluded the way to do this was through low prices, and this was the genesis of a company that now has over 1,000 stores worldwide, aims for 3,000,[1] and controls its entire supply chain from manufacturing to retail.[2]

Nitori has become the leader in its field in Japan, but Akio Nitori himself was quick to realize, as Dhirubhai Ambani had done, that pursuit of profit alone would not be the engine for success. "Before going to the US, I thought revenue and profit first," he says. Afterwards, he thought, "Focus on improving Japanese lives. Revenue comes as a result. Revenue and profits shouldn't be the goal." And if revenue doesn't come, it means the customer wasn't satisfied, he says.

bigger, and it is frequently a belief that what they do elevates their society. They balance their drive for results and achievement with a strong recognition that they are in it for the long haul and that something as big as societal influence takes generations to play out. This, more than anything, is what differentiates the founder from the professional.

In this trailblazing respect, founders – who have brought their enterprises into existence, nurtured them, married their lives and fortunes to them – tend to think quite differently to professional CEOs. "You can never expect a CEO to have the same kind of emotion, attachment, and commitment as entrepreneurs," says Jeffrey Li at GL Capital, who as the Founder of a China-based private equity firm and a former professional China CEO of Novartis has a front-row seat to observe the way these leaders behave.

"Entrepreneurs are the owners, no question about it. And when you are the owner your motivation is different to CEOs."

Being Different to Solve a Problem

With this longer time frame and sense of purpose in mind, founders find it natural to attempt something different. There is a great novelty and purpose in creating something that simply didn't exist before. But they do so to solve a problem, often making a contribution not only for their stakeholders but also for their country.

David Ku was 40 years old when he founded WeBank in Shenzhen in 2014, and had spent 13 years at Ping An witnessing the growth of the country and the financial needs of its individuals. This had taught him that there was a large group of people being ignored by the existing financial services industry, and he set out to serve them without any clear targets for size or profitability. This gave him his niche.

"I wanted to do something different," he says. "And I believed there should be something different. That's the very simple starting point."

When WeBank was founded it was a pioneer as a digital bank in Asia, analogous to a digital bank in the US, using social media and other big data to approve credit loans in seconds. More specifically, Ku's vision is "better banking for all," serving the mass market and small and medium-sized enterprises, and looking for innovative and technology-backed solutions to find ways to serve people whom it was previously not profitable to address.

He hopes that "people will say, 'Wow, they built it. That's something great.'"

The same principle of serving the unserved by doing something different applied at the foundation of HDFC Bank in India. For sure, Founder Aditya Puri could see a gap in the market – foreign banks had products and services, nationalized banks had brand and funding, but nobody had both – but there was also a sense that serving a financially under-penetrated market would also be a significant step toward a better India. "Substitute the money lender. Take banking beyond the urban areas," Puri says. And give the unbanked a world-class service. "That was the main purpose. And as to whether we thought we would make money, the answer was no, none of us thought so. That wasn't the primary intention."

Another who sought to be first was Nykaa Founder Falguni Nayar, who had been influenced by the systems of entrepreneurial decision-making she had encountered at Kotak Mahindra, and particularly Uday Kotak's spirit of "the road less traveled."

"I was convinced that beauty was underrepresented in India, and I wanted to build a beauty industry in India," she says. She wanted to marry specialty beauty retailing with e-commerce, despite others telling her that e-commerce was better attempted through electronics and fashion. "Sometimes that road less traveled, or having the courage of conviction in your decision that this is the right industry to build, makes a lot of difference."

But she knew what she built had to be new. "Some of the success and early recognition comes from doing something different and doing it for the first time."

Founders are looking forward to new ways to be different. Ambani believes that if India continues to import 80% of its energy its future growth may not be sustainable, so he is committing investment today to make India a net energy exporter over the next 10 years. This, as much as commercial aptitude, will guide his positioning in the sector – though he will certainly be expecting to make a return from it.

Seeking the Unique

In Kazakhstan, Kaspi Founder Mikhail Lomtadze shares Ku's desire to be something more than what is available today. "We really wanted to do something more than just be a bank," he says. "There are very few people who love banks." He wanted to create a company with the mission to improve people's lives by developing innovative mobile services. His solution was to create a super app, which is now a leader across multiple verticals. "That was the main driver: to create something unique."

Itaru Tanimura also uses the word *unique* to describe not only M3's ambitions but also the mission statement itself. Rather than something generic like "for the customers" that could apply to any company, he wanted something specific. Here's what he came up with: M3's mission is making use of the internet to increase, as much as possible, the number of people who can live longer and healthier lives, and to reduce, as much as possible, the amount of unnecessary medical costs. To turn this into something rather more catchy, they came up with medicine, media, and metamorphosis – hence the company name, M3.

As well as explaining to any employee or investor what the company actually does, Tanimura found this extremely helpful in giving them something to pilot toward. "The mission was designed to clarify why we were establishing the company, what we and our staff would dedicate our lives to, and to make it" – that word again – *unique*.

"It's an endless pursuit – whether it's increasing the number of people impacted or reducing costs by even one yen, it's something we can continue indefinitely."

Passing a Mission Between Generations: Mahindra & Mahindra

Anand Mahindra, whose grandfather and grand-uncle founded Mahindra & Mahindra, came to the company in 1991. During several years of what he calls "hard yards" of business process reengineering, facing the unions, building productivity, surviving the changes that came with India's liberalization, and selling floors of its office building to make money, he found himself too busy to think much of vision and purpose. He was in a similar frame of mind to Lou Gerstner during his time as CEO of IBM when he said, "I don't have time for vision right now." "I was in a similar mode," says Anand, who became Vice Chairman in 1997, "but people started saying, 'What's the way forward?' And it was about time to do that."

Initially he found the idea of defining purpose difficult, fearing that many companies pay lip service to the idea by grafting it on conveniently to what they were already doing. Then his human resources department unearthed the first ever ad Mahindra & Mahindra had published following its foundation as a steel trading company in 1945.[3]

It spoke of a number of the characteristics we have identified in modern founders' missions. They included nation building ("a coordinated scheme to develop India's resources and raise the standard of living of the masses") and specific principles such as the encouragement of private enterprise, the initiative of the individual, labor rights, confidence, and an acceptance that "ability is the sole test of advancement and neither colour, creed nor a caste should stand in the way."

Reading this, Anand realized that his predecessors had done his work for him: that there was already treasure in the house and there was no need to go searching for it or its meaning. "I inherited a company that was created out of vision. We were created for a purpose."

"I'm just going back to the future. This is not reinventing anything. We just have to live up to what the founding fathers wanted."

Chapter Two

I Have Insatiable Hunger to Build

"I have almost no rest."

—Akio Nitori, Nitori Holdings

Asia's founders are characterized by rare drive. They always want to do more and never consider their mission complete. They are pushed by a desire to reinvent, to grow, to recalibrate for ever greater ambitions.

An example of this restless energy at work is Kiran Mazumdar-Shaw's reinvention of Biocon, which has changed focus several times in the years since its foundation.

"I believe very firmly in the power of science and technology as an entrepreneur," she says. "I pursue that ethos in a very differentiated way, saying, 'What can I do next?'"

It was this ethos that took her from a focus on enzymes – initially a plant enzyme extracted from papaya – to recombinant DNA–based biopharmaceuticals, to monoclonal antibodies, and finally biosimilars. For the nonscientist, these distinctions may not be clear, but each one has been a reinvention and a refusal to settle for what has always been achieved.

"I have always tried to challenge the status quo," she says. "I've always tried to differentiate and I've always chosen science."

"When you're doing something very new which nobody else has tried out, you have to innovate yourself into treading on that new path," she says. "When you challenge yourself on the path of differentiation, it's amazing how you can innovate."

An example is her development of recombinant human insulin, used in the treatment of diabetes. She did this because no such product was available in India; instead, animal insulins were used because they were cheaper. It is because of those absences that she did pioneering work. "And today it's the most affordable insulin anywhere in the world, because I disrupted the space." Others have since reduced their own prices. "It's a 100-year-old molecule. Why should it be so expensive? That was the question I was asking."

* * *

Founders don't let themselves be deterred by adversity. If they are knocked back in their attempt to achieve a missionary objective, they regroup and try again.

An example of this against-the-odds fortitude is CP Group's Senior Vice Chairman Suphachai Chearavanont's experience of taking over a telecoms concession in Thailand in 2011. The concession's efforts to use a newly acquired frequency for 3G were blocked by the regulator after the group had raised funds and rolled out 30% of intended coverage. "Everyone around me said to stop. Don't move forward," he recalls. "But I asked myself, do the Thai people deserve 3G?" There was no 3G in Thailand at the time.

Today he says it was the missionary intent of the business that drove his decision. "When you face a really difficult decision – go or no go for the business, whether to stop, dissolve, or sell – you have to ask, if you continue, can you create value for society? If you believe so, that's the critical point." The whole country did then move to 3G. "My experience taught me: if you do the right thing for the market and for people, the rest is minor – even if you take personal risks. If you invest and operate in a country, the people of the country must benefit, and then the company can benefit."

Chapter Three

I Succeed If My Nation and Community Succeed

"Our employees, business partners, shareholders, and even competitors are all resources."

—Takahisa Takahara, Unicharm

There is a truism of business and investment: that a rising tide lifts all boats. We can apply this to how founders think about stakeholders and the ecosystem within which they operate.

The phrase stakeholder capitalism refers to a business model in which a company considers the interests of all stakeholders – so not just shareholders but also employees, customers, suppliers, government, and the community within which they operate – as they go about building their business. This is distinct from a more shareholder-focused view of value creation, and in theory in the longer term it creates even more value, but distributes it more widely and in a sustainable manner for all involved.

It's worth looking closely at this premise as it relates to founders. There is an argument that their extremely long-term view and clear-sighted sense of where they are going suits stakeholder capitalism very well. While sharing wealth may not be the motive of founders, they do understand they live in an interdependent world and that their success depends on others.

"I understood very early that, without stakeholders' active encouragement and support, Infosys would not be able to move successfully towards its vision," says Narayana Murthy, who founded the world-leading IT company in 1981. "I also realized that, in every collaboration and transaction, it is important to take decisions that will benefit both Infosys and the concerned stakeholder."

Building a Business for a National Need

Stakeholder capitalism, viewed correctly, applies not just to immediate partners and investors but also the fortunes of a nation. The idea of national elevation has often influenced founder decisions to go into new sectors that they might not have considered without some sense of social impact.

A national or social ambition can be very much aligned with a corporate one. Ho Hung Anh, who has been Chairman of the Vietnamese bank Techcombank since 2008,[1] seeks to build a top 10 bank in Southeast Asia, and believes that doing so will galvanize the financial health of Vietnam itself. He aims to build a bank that "brings the best value for the community," while also doing something constructive to develop Vietnam's capital markets to ensure avenues of capital-raising for growing enterprises.

Today, banks in Vietnam do support business development, but through direct lending and the money markets rather than debt and equity, and Ho sees it as a role of banks themselves to change this for the good of the nation. "The role of banks in Vietnam will be very critical in growing and developing the country," he says, both in supporting citizens and empowering Vietnamese companies to grow.

So Ho's purpose requires aiming above corporate growth. "You can't just look at the personal interest or a company's interests," he says. "First, you need to look at the success of the country, and if the country is healthy, then the business is healthy and citizens are healthy. And when businesses and retail customers are healthy, then it will bring the biggest returns to the shareholders. That's the way I prioritize my goal."

Vietnam's growing population – over 100 million people in a demographic sweet spot with an emerging affluent middle class – fit both the banking ambition and the national one. "Bringing the best value to the citizens and business: I think all governments in the world will be supportive of that idea. No regulator would not support that."

"If your goal is to benefit your country and your citizens, your people, then it's not very difficult."

Sidney Lu felt a similar sense of nation-building possibility in 1990 while he was working at AMP (now known as TE Connectivity) in the United States, enjoying a lucrative career in American tech, when he had a conversation with Terry Gou, who had founded Hon Hai Precision in Taiwan in 1974. AMP at the time was a US$5 billion company, Hon Hai about US$60 million, so a move from one to the other seemed a curious step. "But Terry convinced me in a very simple way," Sidney says.

"He said, 'Look around the connector industry. Among the world's top 10 companies, 7 are from the United States and 3 are from Japan. Where is Taiwan?'" Hon Hai was the largest in Taiwan but didn't crack the top 50 globally.

Hon Hai means vast ocean, and that sense of scale was something Gou expressed and Lu embraced. Gou asked Lu, "Do you want to build something here?" Lu was sold, and made the move, founding what is known today as Foxconn Interconnect Technology.

Putting Taiwan on the semiconductor map gave him drive. "That sense of mission . . . . I'm the first in the office every day at 5.30 a.m." And it is notable that others in his sector were galvanized by a similar sense of mission: the biggest of all semiconductor companies, TSMC, was founded by Morris Chang, who had a highly successful leadership role at Texas Instruments before moving to Taiwan, and at age 56, built a new world leader in semiconductors.

Bajaj and a Mission Anchored in History

The Bajaj Group conglomerate has its roots in some pivotal Indian history: the family business hit 100 years of operations in 2026. Jamnalal Bajaj, who founded the group, was so close to Mahatma Gandhi that Gandhi referred to Jamnalal as his fifth son; Jamnalal devoted himself to Gandhi's freedom movement and both men believed India must create its own industry as a solution to reducing poverty.

Jamnalal's great grandson, Sanjiv, who serves as Chairman and Managing Director of Bajaj Finserv, wears this history with some pride. "Gandhi stayed as our guest the last 10 years of his life in our hometown, Wardha, after he moved out of Gujarat. My grandfather Kamalnayan fought for India's independence and was a member of the first three parliaments of India. So nation building has always been important: Gandhi used to say we need more Indians to build domestic businesses while also contributing to social good."

"In everything we do, we see how we are building high-quality, competitive businesses which also contribute to society. Doing good business can also be good for society."

At Ayala Corporation in the Philippines, they've been aligning with the country for 191 years: Ayala's very first investments in the mid-1800s were firsts for the country at the time, from a distillery to a pharmacy to a streetcar system in Old Manila. A key factor in the company's longevity "has been to stay relevant to the changing nature of the country and the economic environment – adapting the institution to new norms and needs rather than sticking to old models," says Jaime Augusto Zóbel de Ayala, Chairman of Ayala Corporation and the seventh generation of a remarkable dynasty. Even the companies from which they have divested endure to "continue to transform the Philippine economy," he says.

Just like the Ambanis, the Ayalas have long found nation building to be lucrative. The Ayala conglomerate covers real estate, banking, telecommunications, power, water, education, and plenty else additionally – all sectors that benefit from a wealthier population and a more robust economy. They've consistently understood a quid pro quo: aim to make a better Philippines and you will build a better business, too. And perhaps their history – founded during Spanish colonization, refined through American colonization, then unleashed into an independent state a year before India in 1946[2] – has been a part of this drive to do more.

We find another example of national alignment in Thailand. "As a Thai company and a Thai citizen, it is our duty to support the Thai economy to the fullest extent of our abilities," says Sarath Ratanavadi, Founder and CEO of Gulf Development. In support of the Thai economy, society, and government, he speaks of "exchanging ideas on how to make Thailand a better place for the young people," and to build "a sustainable future for the next generation." Gulf's growth and Thailand's go together, he says. Since 2000, Thailand's gross installed capacity has aligned with the growth of the country's GDP.

Narayana Murthy and Treating Stakeholders with Respect

The son of a teacher in a lower-middle-class family, Narayana Murthy of Infosys believes very strongly in fairness and respect – "my vision was to make Infosys India's most respected company" – and tried from the outset to apply those values within his ecosystem.

For example, in seeking higher respectability from government, he understood the government's objectives: higher exports, more jobs, better taxes, and national prosperity. To contribute toward that vision, Murthy and his team created jobs, paid taxes, practiced good governance, and gained respect for honesty from bureaucrats.[3] As well as being the right thing to do, he thought it would be good for business. "My belief has been that pursuing respect will bring success in all business parameters."

When interviewed, Murthy constantly used the word *respect* as he talks about the many people with whom he interacts. "Respect from the stakeholders is the most important requirement for a corporation to

Stakeholder Complexity

Many businesses featured in this book operate in extremely complex and interconnected environments. A key skill is to map out stakeholders comprehensively, work out the various patterns between them, and make stakeholder impact a key part of any business case.

For Thailand's CP Group, for example, that means partnership with government, farmers, communities, nongovernmental organizations, suppliers, and retailers. For Gulf Development, it means not only an understanding of the hopes of the government and the needs of the consumer but also the achieve enduring economic success," he says. Customers? "If you want respect from a customer, you will earn the customer's trust by delivering what you promised on time, within budget and exceeding the expected quality." Employees? "To earn respect you must be fair, transparent and accountable in every transaction with them."

In managing his ecosystem, Murthy used adages such as the following:

- When in doubt, disclose.
- In God I trust and everybody else has to bring data to the table.
- The softest pillow is a clear conscience.
- Let the good news take the stairs but ensure the bad news takes the elevator.

These are, fundamentally, matters of transparency and disclosure – to the market, to the board, to the team – but they have at their heart a philosophy of straight dealing with the ecosystem and a belief that doing so leads to better and more sustainable growth for his own company and those who interact with it.

policy priorities of the regulator. In countries like South Korea, where HD Hyundai Electric and GS Caltex operates, it will involve navigating complex stakeholder relationships at both the company and industry levels.

There is a skill to identifying where within an ecosystem to get involved: trying to influence everything is scattershot and pointless. "We make an effort only within our circle of control," says Jeffrey Li at GL Capital. "We don't waste time thinking about anything outside that circle of influence. For example, we just take geopolitical risk as a new norm."

Everything at Asian founder-led companies starts with mission – something that gives them a reason for what they do and a compass to steer

How Midea Partnered to Take on the World

A crucial element of stakeholder capitalism is partnership: the recognition that one company can't do everything, and will be greatly assisted if it finds partners who can help with gaps in distribution, product, and technology. China's Midea gives us a clear example of using partnership to elevate its ambitions.

In 2017, Midea set about an evolution in what it wanted to be. From focusing on manufacturing as a home appliance specialist, it aimed for something bigger: to be a builder of the smart home service ecosystem.

Midea's Chairman Fang Hongbo, who succeeded Midea Founder He Xiangjian in 2013, calls this "an industry ecosystem of two-way empowerment." He also uses the phrase "you in me, and me in you," a "business model that has formed a solid community of shared interests, accelerating the prosperity of the entire ecosystem."

This is quite a common idea – that working together to build a bigger market benefits everyone within it – but what does it mean in practice? For Midea, it starts with partnership: with leading smartphone companies, internet platform companies, and smart automobile enterprises.

But the greatest expression of Fang's ecosystem commitment is not as visible as products in stores: it is digital. In 2016 Midea began to look at

with in getting there. As well as providing them with a sense of worth and social utility, it's also very beneficial as a business practice: it forces a healthy long-term view, it provides a useful lens through which to view new opportunities, and it also tends to make for very profitable high-growth businesses even if the framing for the vision is about neither. Everything that follows in this book builds on mission.

exporting solutions and set up Midea Cloud (Meiyun Zhishu) based on Midea's own digital transformation experience. It started by serving Midea's own supply chain, upstream and downstream; now, it serves more than 5,000 of these enterprises, and another 1,000 medium and large enterprises across 50 sectors from automobile manufacturing to food, cement, energy, and electronics. The M.IoT Industrial Internet Platform, built out of Midea Cloud in 2018, has empowered over 600,000 industrial enterprises.

That's a remarkable reach, but it's much easier if all these businesses can connect with one other, so Midea took a proactive step and set about creating technical standards to enable enterprises and industry associations to interconnect. It has worked with the Ministry of Industry and Information Technology to establish the Manufacturing Industry AIGC Application Standard, which builds a framework for data governance, knowledge accumulation, and scenario implementation.

Through careful and dynamic management of its own ecosystem, and the shrewd selection of partners, Midea has grown from a single-industry, single-brand company in a small township into a global technology group across multiple brands and industries.

Reflective Questions

Driven by Mission

1. What is the mission you are on and what is driving it?
2. How are you navigating different stakeholders to deliver against your mission and for your society?
3. How are you developing missionary zeal in your next generation of leaders?

A Telescope in One Eye, a Microscope in the Other

"When the world looks bleak, this is where we find our best opportunity."

—Nicholas Moore, Macquarie

Governing Mindsets

- **I sense constantly and bet on long-term megatrends.**
- **I have no long term without the short term.**

In September 2008, the global financial crisis (GFC) turned its full wrath on Macquarie Bank.[1] Volatility and unrest had been accelerating for months amid fears of a crunch in the credit markets, and after Lehman Brothers collapsed on September 15, the market seemed to decide the Australian financial services group was next. Within five trading days its share price fell 40%[2] while credit default swaps on its subordinated debt widened from 200 to 1,800 basis points, inferring an expectation of default. Counterparties began to refuse to deal with Macquarie, sensing the end was nigh.

But it would later turn out that even then, even as CEO Nicholas Moore had huddled his core team in a makeshift war room on Sydney's Martin Place, even as he sought endlessly to reassure regulators and investors that the bank's liquidity was fine, even as he made the case to a doubting market for the institution's very survival, Macquarie was bidding for a troubled asset in America that would, 13 years later, propel it to record profits.

Half a world away Constellation Energy, a Baltimore-based energy major that had hit a liquidity crisis, announced plans to sell its downstream gas operations in Houston. Macquarie at the time had a modest energy trading operation in the United States – Macquarie Cook – and could see a great opportunity in Constellation: it would complete the bank's US footprint, giving the operation scale and 100 new excellent people, a far bigger team than they already had.

But the timing? To be able to even think of such an acquisition as the world's media wrote of your impending demise and counterparties closed their doors? Remarkably, Macquarie's acquisition of Constellation Energy was announced in February 2009, a month before Macquarie's GFC share price low.

"We know historically that when the world looks bleak, this is often where we find our best opportunity," says Moore, who was CEO and Managing Director for 10 years from 2008, concluding a career there that lasted 32 years. "When the world was looking grim in 2008, 2009, [and] 2010, we were continuously asking: there's great opportunities out there. Bring us good ideas."

And it paid off. Years later, in 2021, Macquarie Group – which had very much survived the GFC because of years of careful planning for funding – would announce a turnaround, from warning of a full-year decline in group profits to projecting a record year. It did so because of a huge boost from that specific US commodities business.[3] Macquarie's acquisition of Constellation remains an extraordinary example of being able to think about the short and the long term simultaneously, to pay equal attention to the telescope and the microscope.

Leading Asian founder-entrepreneurs know where they're going: it might take years, sometimes decades to get there, but there's no doubting their ability to keep a watchful eye on the compass.

Reaching their intended destination, though, is rarely some steady linear journey mapped by an obedient GPS. Even the greatest founder-led companies have had to navigate numerous unexpected diversions on their way to their achievements, with wrong turns, dead ends, and closed roads along the way.

They'll still get there, though, because they know how to keep their eye on that destination while paying careful attention to the state of the road right in front of them.

Chapter Four

I Sense Constantly and Bet on Long-Term Megatrends

"I realized that something extraordinary was going to happen."
—Narayana Murthy, Infosys

Let's start with the telescope.

The key skill that separates founders from their peers is their ability to spot a distant trend and to align with it in good time to benefit.

We have all become used to the idea of the megatrend: digitalization, urbanization, climate, the healthcare needs of aging societies, geopolitical fractures and artificial intelligence (AI). But founders see these things before others do. Seeing the future is only one part of the equation, though: what's equally important is to place the correct bets to benefit from them over the very long term.

Reliance Industries, for example, has done this since its foundation in 1957. Dhirubhai Ambani began trading in spices and other goods, but from the outset was looking for new opportunities, for signs of a future to align with. He found one in polyester, which had been introduced in America in 1951 and by 1960 was beginning to attract attention elsewhere in the world. Dhirubhai saw a gap in trading this new synthetic, but in a characteristic step, he looked beyond what was possible today and instead set about pursuing tomorrow. He moved into production, set up world-scale capacities and sought to export to establish global competitiveness.

"If you follow Reliance, you'll see that we reinvent a business every three, four, five years – always evolving," says Mukesh Ambani. He calls it "chasing the future," and seeks to extrapolate what that future might look like 20 years or more out and apply it to decisions today. "We don't limit ourselves to just what seems realistic in the present. Today's Reliance is a completely different Reliance, because the world changes every 5 or 10 years. Many times we've changed with the world."

This enterprising spirit requires a certain mindset. "That's been Reliance's DNA: we will figure it out as long as we have the right talent and the right goal," says Ambani. "We always say, 'If you focus on the obstacles you'll never reach your goal. But if you focus on the goal you will overcome all obstacles.'" A fine example of this came in the 1980s, when challenges with port development in India caused Reliance to rethink its supply issues for ethylene. The solution – to transfer the ethylene from a big carrier to a smaller one mid-sea, not at the port – was a world-first innovation to solve an irksome problem. It was a solution that required a telescope trained on a distant vision.

Today, for example, Reliance has three artificial intelligence platforms in development, and Ambani seeks to be a world leader in the field. It will take time, but he knows where he's going. "If you're not doing something that's never been done before, what's the point?"

Mapping for Megatrends

Enterprises that thrive are the ones that see the future and position accordingly, and many of our interviewees are among the best at doing so.

When David Ku set up WeBank, the first thing he had to do was develop an extremely clear view on the trends that would shape his institution. Some were obvious: growing digital acceptance and the use of the mobile phone. Some were at the state level: a pro-innovation, pro-growth country with a growing economy and a population of consumers wanting greater inclusion within banking. Some were regulatory, and therefore subject to change: a sense that the government would pay more attention to the mass market and that the need to serve the underserved would likely lead to a benign regulatory environment.

Only after mapping this out did Ku feel ready to set course. "We said, 'Okay, if we really want to build something great, we cannot go against any of these trends,'" he says.

Number one, they would be digital. Number two, they would focus on serving the neglected – small and medium-sized enterprises and mass market customers – in hope of the greatest possible regulatory and government support. So far so good: as the future Ku positioned for steadily arrives, WeBank is logging over 30% return on equity.[1]

At Singapore's UOB, third-generation leader Wee Ee Cheong had spotted a megatrend of his own: the inexorable rise of ASEAN.[2] UOB has 90 years of history in Singapore and has been extremely successful, but that's a relatively small-population market, though sophisticated. Wee has long advocated for greater heft in his surrounding region, for good reason: ASEAN has a 686 million population,[3] much of it young, with attractive gross domestic product growth and a strong outlook.

The problem was that growing in ASEAN through organic growth would have taken too long, and so an outsize bet was required to match the trend. The opportunity presented itself in 2021, with the COVID-19 pandemic still raging, when Citibank announced it was exiting consumer businesses in markets all over Asia. Wee knew that if he could persuade Citi to sell four key businesses in one block – in Malaysia, Indonesia, Thailand, and Vietnam – there was a chance to transform in an instant.

Given the pandemic, it was a very tough call. "I thought very hard," he says now. "It was a time of crisis: we don't know what's going to happen, nobody knows. It could be glass half full or half empty."

"But I thought: maybe this is the best time for us, because if we want to build a consumer business in ASEAN, we need scale." He knew the market might be against him, but he had been around long enough not to be distracted by noise. "If I want to listen to analysts and drive my share price up, then my behavior would be different," he says.

Instead, he forced himself to look as far ahead as possible. "You cannot have a short-term view. If you are too short term in nature, you can't move," he says. And so he went ahead, with the purchase announced in January 2022.

"You have to take a view, otherwise you end up very piecemeal and transactional," he says. "I think this would differentiate the owner-operator model from the pure professional. They would just look at a number. We have to be forward looking, stay the course, and hopefully, over the long-term, we will be much better."

It's true that, as a member of the controlling family,[4] he had time and security on his side, which made it an easier call to make than it might have been for a professional CEO. But Wee was guided by the fact that his responsibility as a steward was to look far ahead and be ready.

"There is 90 years of history in the bank. I want to make it 100 and beyond."

Aligning with a National Megatrend

Two other examples show the value of spotting a megatrend at the domestic level. Back in 1985, that's exactly what Uday Kotak was doing as he set up a new kind of financial services firm in India.

Kotak was watching India navigate that cusp point when the country began to move from Nehru's socialism to a steady opening up of the economy. Seeking opportunity within that generational trend, he didn't have to look very far. "By far the biggest opportunity was a very imperfect financial sector marketplace," he says.

Imperfect was the word: he recalls banks would take deposits at 6% at the time, and the lending rate was fixed by the central bank at 17%, irrespective of the quality of the borrower – a 1,100 basis point spread.

Clearly that couldn't last, and opportunities would emerge from the reinvention of the sector, but it still raised the question of how to position. In setting up his own shop, he already had the distinct founder advantage of time: Kotak only speaks of a medium-term view (he thinks the world is changing too fast to speak of a long-term one) but even that was an advantage over the hired professional CEOs commonplace in Indian banking, whose tenure is set by the regulator at three years, with renewals subject to the board and the Reserve Bank of India.

That meant he could plan far ahead as befits such a long-term trend. But he also knew that if he was to build for something that might take decades to play out, he had to have the correct processes in place.

Kotak has also learned to differentiate between noise and insight. "I have this saying: be very careful that the lessons of history do not become the baggage of history," he says. "The Asian crisis, securities scandal,[5] and global financial crisis gave us great lessons. But you don't carry baggage, and the line between conviction and foolhardiness is very thin."

He is the first to admit he has not always got that right, making a short-term decision to slow down expansion of Kotak Mahindra's distribution network during the turmoil of the global financial crisis when in retrospect he should have doubled down and been bolder. Being far-sighted isn't a guarantee of being right.

Twenty years after Kotak launched his firm, Ho Hung Anh was in another country at a pivotal moment: Vietnam.

Ho knew that in building Techcombank, he was aligning himself with Vietnam's attempts to transform itself into a high-population middle-class nation. That was the easy bit. "It is not very difficult to figure out where long-term opportunities lie, but what is important is that you have an aspiration to deliver against those opportunities."

This involves aiming high. Ho felt that a mediocre ambition would lead to short-term goals and modest outcomes. "But if we believe that we can be like Japan or South Korea, we see there is a long way to go and there are a lot of long-term opportunities. We need to figure out our pathway to that destination, that peak."

Every one of these founder-entrepreneurs had to think of the short term, too, and did so adeptly. But it all started with being able to spot the long-term trend and position for it.

Chapter Five

I Have No Long Term Without the Short Term

"Don't assume the game will stay the same."

—Djohan Emir Setijoso, BCA

Now for the microscope.

We have observed the acute sensing ability founders have for the long-term trend. But they know that the long term won't exist without paying sufficient attention to the short term: the day-to-day needs of the business.

The short term enables the long term. It's making the money day by day to allow a transformational investment in a megatrend. It's studying what's happening in costs and earnings to ensure that the business is in tight enough shape for the founder to do what they want to do over the next 10 years.

The skill of founder-entrepreneurs is to hold these thoughts together simultaneously, despite the vast difference in time frame, and to balance seamlessly between the two. Achieving it requires further acts of delicate equilibrium: being bold in the pursuit of new opportunities while being fastidious on risk, operating across multiple geographies and sectors within a diverse portfolio of interests to achieve the desired outcome. The balanced founder might be chasing a trend that will serve them well until 2050, but they will also be thinking: how do we launch this new app in the next three weeks? Show me a project plan for what will be done day by day. And the short-term actions, aggregated, all advance them in the direction of the long-term results.

"You must learn to both perform for today and transform for tomorrow," says Sanjiv Bajaj, Chairman and Managing Director of Bajaj Finserv. Many companies in the Bajaj Group are listed with quarterly earnings requirements, and that requires immediate attention with a commensurate level of scrutiny. But that never dims his focus on the horizon. "Whenever you have to make a choice about something that will bring a short-term gain but will hurt you in the long term, choose the long-term option," he says.

A Balancing Act of Time

The short term and long term are not two isolated and unrelated positions. One leads directly to the other, and the smart founder will realize that a decision made under time pressure today to effect an immediate change will ripple through the future of the company.

For Ho Hung Anh to navigate the megatrend of Vietnam's emergence, he first had to consider short-term challenges. One was funding. Domestic capital markets are undeveloped and there isn't enough long-term inbound investment into those markets to support it. "Vietnam is not a market where capital accumulation has been strong enough for us to take longer rides, and we cannot raise very long-term sources of funding to create value far in the future," he says.

He therefore had to build capital internally in order to get the financial fortitude to chase Vietnam's demographic and economic potential. He couldn't do one without the other. "We need to simultaneously try to build our capital but at the same time think about the future," he says. If investors won't commit long-term capital, "we need to rely on ourselves."

Achieving the correct balance is a skill. "You have to be courageous somewhere, and you have to be cautious somewhere," says Falguni Nayar at Nykaa. "It's not just all caution, and it's not just all aggression. It's a balance." Her view on risk was shaped by her time in banking at Kotak Mahindra, which helped her understand the balance between immediate gains and investing for the future. "I've learned that I was okay to make investment and lose money in the short term. But the path to unit economics needed to be right so that you were building a business that would make money in the long run."

Sarath Ratanavadi, founder of Gulf Development in Thailand, has learned plenty about the need for balance and the short-term decisions needed to effect a long-term goal. Gulf Development's initial intention was to set up 700 MW coal-fired power stations, a long-term view (all infrastructure, after all, is long term). During the development phase, the company encountered concerns from local communities, which led to a quick switch to a gas and renewable energy–focused power producer with a strict no-coal policy.[1] So this was a decision made in the short term but with very long-term consequences.

"We became more mindful of our impact and took a more sustainable approach from the start," Ratanavadi says. In doing so, Gulf moved ahead of the game – not just by setting ambitious renewables targets such as 40% renewables by 2035 but also by achieving that target five years early.[2]

Bank Central Asia and Building from Wreckage

Djohan Emir Setijoso's role in rebuilding Bank Central Asia (BCA) after its recapitalization by the Indonesian state during the 1997 Asian financial crisis (see footnote[3] for background) is a classic example of being able to manage the short and long term simultaneously.

Setijoso was expected to build a bank good enough to emerge from state control back into public listing, something robust enough to thrive for the future, but at the same time he was trying to stabilize it amid a debilitating crisis that had hit BCA worse than most.

So his first short-term task was stability. "It's hard to imagine now, but there were 700 or 800 people crowding around the ATMs at our office," he says. He asked people to be calm, not to be afraid. He remembers one saying to him, "You can say that, but this is my money."

"This is why trust is critical," Setijoso says – trust of customers and employees alike. Getting that trust back immediately was a matter of survival. "Without trust, the bank has no liquidity. Without liquidity, there's no trust. It's a vicious circle. And liquidity is the oxygen for a bank: without it, you faint in minutes, the bank collapses."

To stop that problem, he made another short-term decision. He asked the relevant state institutions to give a clear statement to employees that the government wanted BCA to continue operating and had no plans to liquidate it. That helped. He lifted a restriction on big corporate customers withdrawing the funds, because the lock-up looked bad: it

"Our vision is long term, yet delivering on it requires disciplined short-term execution," he says. "Otherwise we won't make it to the long term. Because the road along the way could be difficult."

suggested a bank unable to repay. But he persuaded them to maintain a static balance voluntarily, another vital short-term measure.

At the same time as this minute-to-minute firefighting, Setijoso was also trying to plan for the long term. He knew that a condition of the International Monetary Fund's support of Indonesia was that the banks wouldn't stay under public control for long, and that there was an urgency to return them to the markets and some degree of private sector ownership. So for the future, he set about tackling institution building, governance, and risk management.

Then, when the Hartonos became interested in BCA, that required another transition – institutional to family-run again – and Setijoso wanted to guide them on the sort of long-term owners they should be. "At that time, big banks weren't seen as profit centers; they were seen as financing centers for their owners' ventures," Setijoso says. But he was convinced the bank could be a very profitable venture on its own. Fortunately, the Hartonos were aligned with that vision.

From this journey of long-term direction and short-term fixing, Setijoso feels he has learned the importance of adaptability. "Experience creates wisdom and intuition, but experience can also imprison your mind," he says. "Success is never permanent. It only exists at the moment you're successful; it doesn't guarantee future success. When things are good, don't be complacent. Don't assume the game will stay the same."

Building Short-Term Apparatus into Megatrends

It is intoxicating to identify a transformational megatrend and to place the bets to benefit for a long-term opportunity. But the best founders are quick to build the correct apparatus behind the scenes to ensure that short-term performance and process is not undermined by the effort.

For Wee Ee Cheong, even as he repositioned the bank for its bold acquisition with its multi-decade time horizon, he was thinking of the short term in two specific ways. He knew that making an acquisition at a time of turmoil would allow him to analyze the accounts to gain a very

Communicate with Investors for the Long Term

For any founder or owner with a listed business, it's essential to communicate with shareholders about both the short and the long term. Investors will tend to forgive a quarterly setback if they understand a well-articulated plan that will pay off years ahead. They will be less tolerant if they feel in the dark.

Nevertheless, some founders actively seek investors whose mindset is similar to their own in terms of distant goals. "I focus on investors who have a long-term horizon," says Dilip Shanghvi, Executive Chairman of Indian pharmaceutical company Sun Pharma, which has a notably low level of retail in its shareholder base: Shanghvi's family owns 55% of the company with 20% domestic institutional and 17% foreign institutional, including the Singapore government and several Indian mutual funds and insurance companies.

"We don't want to run the business quarter-to-quarter and we don't want investors to be driven by quarter-to-quarter changes," he says.

good read on the behavior of customers under stress, showing what his new portfolio would look like on the day it became part of UOB.

Also, while the acquisition was underway – and it was cemented in steady and deliberate stages over several years – Wee never lost sight of the overall bank's inherent prudence, with a conservative credit culture managed precisely on a regular short-term basis. UOB has, at the time of writing, a nonperforming loan ratio of just 1.6%, one of the lowest figures in the industry.[4]

In Vietnam, Ho took steps in the short term to fortify his balance sheet for the vast challenge ahead. He did so by creating an appropriate funding mix that, once it navigated the short-term enthusiasms and doubts of the

---

That said, he prefers to work not on a generational time frame but the mid-term. "I don't plan 10 years ahead. I plan two, three years ahead," he says. He has a mental map on which "we are always working on four or five things. How many of them work out decides our cash flow, which changes our ability to do things in the future."

Joseph Tsai, Vice Chairman at Cathay Financial, has to go one step further than quarterly reporting and report numbers on a monthly basis.

"If you're going to stress about the number every month you're never going to get anything done. You would never invest in anything, just to keep the cost down."

In fact, Tsai considers it part of his role to be a counterweight against the team of managers who must look at numbers on a day-to-day basis. To Tsai, it's a responsibility to step back and see the longer term – and to take investors with him. "We've tried to cultivate a conversation with our shareholders and say we are going to look at the longer term," he says. "That's why you would choose us."

---

market, would pay off indefinitely. "In Vietnam, we like to say you need to use the short-term gains to fund the long-term aspiration," he says.

And Uday Kotak had to be extremely nimble in the short term when, following a securities scandal in 1992, the Reserve Bank of India stopped rediscounting of bills by banks for private companies – and bill discounting was 70–75% of Kotak Mahindra's revenue at the time. "Effectively that whole line of business stopped overnight." The bank was forced to learn to pivot quickly and reinvent itself, aided by a nascent car finance business and a broader plan to develop the capital markets, initially in a joint venture with Goldman Sachs. It worked, and Kotak Mahindra continued to align with the Indian liberalization that is now almost half a century underway. Along the way it has become approximately a US$50 billion enterprise.[5]

Trade-Offs on the Way to a Long-Term Goal

The world is unpredictable and the best-laid plans for a long-term vision can be disrupted along the way. The best founders, while keeping their eye on a distant prize, can be nimble in the short term when they have to be. There's no problem with a temporary and necessary change of course provided the compass remains set on the eventual destination.

The most universal example of this in recent times was the COVID-19 pandemic. It caused many founder-entrepreneurs to change their thinking about time frames. The key was how they adapted – and all learned from the experience.

As a healthcare business, M3 was affected more than most; Founder Itaru Tanimura had to shift from his usual long-term perspective to a very short-term set of priorities. As he did so, he learned that investors did not always appreciate the shift.

"The reason was that the challenges were so significant, and with everyone struggling in the healthcare field, we couldn't just sit back and do nothing," he says. "So we paused everything else and focused entirely on COVID-19 measures."

The company mandate became to save as many lives as possible, through as many different means as possible. For example, M3 used its network to find doctors to dispense vaccines in rural areas, administering seven million doses, and conducted clinical trials. They collected and distributed two million masks. Online physician consulting was made free through LINE healthcare (a joint venture between M3 and the Japanese social media app LINE), leading to 40 times as many consultations in February 2020 compared to January.[6] "During that time, we moved quickly, even doing things that weren't profitable. But some initiatives did generate revenue, and our performance skyrocketed."

The stock price also rose significantly – though it subsequently dropped, at one point by 85%, which brought challenges from shareholders and "was a bit of a trial, even mentally."

"Looking back, if I were in the same situation again, I think I'd do the same thing . . . . If anything, I might have communicated to investors that this was a temporary situation and asked them not to factor it into their expectations. But at the time, I didn't do that."

"I learned what happens when you focus entirely on the short term. It reinforced the importance of maintaining a mid- to long-term perspective in business."

The M3 example tells us to adapt to extreme circumstances where necessary, but there are trade-offs involved, particularly with what investors want a company to do. Anchoring on a company's North Star throughout aids them through this period of dislocation.

Reflective Questions

A Telescope in One Eye, a Microscope in the Other

1. How do you continuously sense new megatrends that will disrupt and propel your industry?
2. How are you and your organization maximizing opportunities in the short term?
3. How do you rate yourself and your team on the ability to find the balance between these two opposing viewpoints?

Bold but Bounded

"It's not just all caution, and it's not just all aggression. It's a balance."

—Falguni Nayar, Nykaa

Governing Mindsets

- **I align long-term risk with the scale of ambition.**
- **I move forward if I can live with the worst case.**
- **I make my own luck.**

Manila, 1994. The nine million people who live in the capital of the Philippines[1] are suffering an intolerable water crisis. In the city's east, three quarters of homes don't have continuous supply; some suffer outages of 20 hours at a time. Fewer than 1 in 12 have a sewerage connection.[2] Two thirds of available water is lost to leaks and illegal connections and the agency in charge[3] is so indebted it cannot invest to fix the problem. President Fidel Ramos orders the government to come up with a solution.

The answer is an experimental framework to privatize Manila's water supply under the National Water Crisis Act, passed in 1995. The government offers two concessions, for East and West Manila, which between them will be expected to take over a system that has been neglected, is straining with overpopulation, and on whose success lives will depend.

It was not an obviously appealing opportunity for the Ayala Group, the oldest and largest conglomerate in the country, by then 160 years old and a leader everywhere from retail to real estate, banking to telecommunications. "PPPs[4] were quite new for the Philippines then, and Ayala at the time had no experience in running utilities," recalls Jaime Augusto Zóbel de Ayala, who succeeded his father as President and CEO in 1994, and today serves as Chairman. Ayala was doing just fine across the suite of businesses it understood; at the time it seemed an outlandish financial and reputational risk to commit to a broken sector in which even this diverse leader had no experience.

Yet Ayala bid for, and in 1997 won, the 25-year concession for the East Zone, operating as subsidiary Manila Water. As an illustration of the risk involved, the company that won the West Manila mandate, Maynilad Water Services, had gone bankrupt by 2003, and Manila Water itself struggled for years with the sheer scale of what needed to be fixed. But it worked: Manila Water went from 3.1 million customers in 1997 to 7.5 million in 2022, bringing 24-hour water availability to the entire East Zone and reducing water losses to a global benchmark 13% from 63% when they took over.[5] And as an investment, when Ayala decided it was time to sell in 2020,[6] the proceeds were so plentiful that they anchored the growth of another contrarian and opportunistic business, the ahead-of-its-time financial services wallet GCash.

But none of this was obvious in the 1990s. So why did Ayala take such a risk? "We saw that this was a tremendous opportunity to enhance the quality of life in Manila, and usher the national capital to keep in step with its more progressive neighbors at the time," he says. For a conglomerate, a better-functioning city is universally good for business. Ayala was thinking on a much bigger scale than what his water venture meant in isolation, and considered risk in that broader context.

And behind that civic ambition was a bigger idea: that risk gives you freedom if you know what to do with it. "We view risk management as a strategic enabler," he says. "Rather than use this process to just avoid or mitigate risks, we harness it as an opportunity to create real value for the company." Risks and their attendant opportunities, he says, are assessed in relation to Ayala's business strategy, operational priorities, and long-term objectives. Risk assessment, properly refined with the right people, processes, and technology, is "harnessed as a lens rather than a filter in evaluating investments."

Ayala understood that risk is not just about caution but enabling opportunity. And in this respect, he is representative of a common mindset throughout the people whose stories fill this book.

Chapter Six

I Align Long-Term Risk with the Scale of Ambition

"The bigger your goal, the more you're willing to take risk."
—David Ku, WeBank

There's a curious misapprehension about Asia's great founder-entrepreneurs: that they got where they are through taking bold bets, placing all their chips on a hopeful hand with the brazen attitude of a fortune-favors-the-brave maverick. The outside world tends to see these people as swashbuckling risk-takers who just keep getting their high-stakes bets right.

But this stereotype just doesn't survive inspection. Without question, leading Asian entrepreneurs take risks: what was Mukesh Ambani's decision to push Reliance into Jio Communications, a multi-billion-dollar commitment into a completely new sector, if not a risk? Or Macquarie's intensely scrutinized purchase of Sydney Airport?

Entrepreneurship is fundamentally about risk-taking. But the great skill of founder-entrepreneurs is to weigh that risk correctly, to evaluate worst cases and their impact, and to understand precisely the potential reward. They have the skill to move the odds in their favor, but they do not take existential risks, even if they might look that way.

The paradox of great Asian leaders is that they can look like bet-the-farm daredevils when in fact they are extremely refined experts in risk management. They wear better seat belts so they can accelerate. It is precisely their caution that enables them to be so fearless.

Aggression and Ambition in Asia

Asian founder-led companies tend toward the aggressive, as befits their reputation as drivers of outsize growth. McKinsey data[1] show that the capex-to-revenue ratio of our universe of these companies is about 40% higher than the rest of the world, and 20% higher than Asian non-founder-led companies. This manifests itself most obviously through acquisition: Asian founder-led companies engage in about 20% more mergers and acquisitions (M&A) deals than non-founder-led companies, although it is notable that North American companies have a higher overall appetite for M&A than do those in Asia, partly because there is a higher number of established and entrenched businesses there to acquire.

So we can certainly conclude that fear is not part of the Asian founder lexicon – or that if they do feel fear, it doesn't stop them doing what they want to do. Some of the boldest corporate ambitions ever attempted are among our interviewees. But in each case, these grand conceits were attempted because of the scale of the prize. A calculation was made that the potential for something truly transformational was worth the associated degree of risk.

A standout example can be found in India: Mukesh Ambani's launch of Reliance Jio.

Jio[2] was soft launched in December 2015[3] offering a national mobile telecommunications network across all of India's 22 available telecom circles. It brought 4G[4] services to India, and later 5G, and has anchored a host of other digital-related businesses beyond cellular telecommunications.[5]

This was all untrodden ground for Reliance when it set about investing in the space in 2010 with investments into 4G spectrum licenses and the infrastructure to support them, including 90,000 towers and over 250,000 kilometers of fiber-optic cable. The spend was colossal: from 2010 to 2016 it deployed almost US$9 billion of investment through Reliance Industries – US$2.2 billion of debt guarantees and US$6.7 billion of equity[6] – alongside US$10–12 billion of debt financing from Indian and international banks. The market was not entirely convinced: Kotak Securities attributed a zero value to Jio when arriving at a target price for Reliance Industries in a research report in 2016.[7]

"The biggest risk we took was with Jio," says Mukesh Ambani, the architect of this bold advance. So why do it? "We've always taken big risks, but we do so with a focus on impact at scale," he says.

For Ambani, it was the size of the prize that made the risk worthwhile – for India itself as much as Reliance. Mukesh told the board that even if it didn't work, if the financials were wrong or if it was too early for India to embrace 4G (and later 5G), "it will still be the best thing we've done for India." And the scale of that opportunity – to digitize what would become the world's most populous nation, to give it a digital edge, to leapfrog its communications – was so big that the reckless approach would have been to ignore it, not to invest in it.

"As opportunities evolve with technology, some of these future-facing opportunities become bigger than our current ones – and we can't ignore them," he says. "That's how we think about risk management."

The investment risk has continued long since the initial commitment to 4G. It is estimated that between 2018 and 2025[8] Reliance invested US$25 billion for the 5G rollout on licenses and physical infrastructure, plus some relevant acquisitions; over the course of 10 years it has also spent US$10–15 billion in next generation digital services, chiefly through acquisitions.

The Bold Bet of Acquisition – Gulf Development and Fubon

One of the biggest steps a company can make is to acquire – especially if that acquisition brings a whole new line of business rather than bolstering an existing one. A good example is Sarath Ratanavadi of Gulf Development, who diversified his business from its focus on energy into telecommunications and data with the acquisition of AIS, a Thai telecom operator,[9] believing that data was not being properly explored as an asset in Thailand.

But perhaps the unique view of the entrepreneur is expressed in the fact that Ratanavadi didn't see the business as all that much of a reach from what he was already doing. "We began to see data usage as similar to the energy business," he says. "A purely data or cloud center is, in essence, a type of infrastructure business." He realized, however, that moving straight from energy to a digital business required "finding a way to bridge the gap."

That's why Gulf Development invested in AIS, which could demonstrate resilient performance, a strong management team, solid cash flows, and the promise of a fruitful partnership. From a risk perspective, that made sense.

While Fubon Group also scaled organically, it is distinctive for its M&A strategy vis-à-vis its peers in Taiwan, and is considered an aggressive acquirer: in addition to expanding its businesses in Taiwan through M&A, the company has made several strategic acquisitions in Mainland China, Hong Kong, South Korea, and Vietnam.

The Jio adventure worked on both of Ambani's relevant matrices, national service, and profitability. First, its proposition was revolutionary to what was previously available: from day one of public launch in 2016 it offered 100% 4G network coverage on mobile phones. The technology was so new for the Indian markets that the company had to offer free service for

Daniel Tsai, Chairman of Fubon Group, learned something of acquisition from the other side: Citigroup's acquisition of a 15% stake in Fubon in stages between 2000 and 2001. "That gave us new capital to replenish what we lost in the Taiwan financial crisis," Daniel says, referring to the local aftermath of the Asian financial crisis, "but the biggest lesson we got from Citi is how they had grown through M&A."

Citi's then leader, Sandy Weill, was a dealmaker who, like the Tsai family, promoted the idea of a financial supermarket. Tsai studied Weill's techniques and, having decided Fubon needed to grow through acquisition rather than just organic growth, put his learnings into practice.

Although outsiders view Fubon as bold and aggressive, Daniel has a different take. "There is a Chinese saying that opportunity is only for people who are ready," he says. "I wouldn't say we were bold. We took calculated risk. We seized the right moment." And after each acquisition they were able to realize synergies.

It's interesting, though, that Fubon was built with an ethos of caution. Daniel's father, Tsai Wan-Tsai, who founded the group, had a series of words he would use as a maxim for employees, and one was *diligence*, which he later changed to *diligence and frugality*.

"The way I interpreted that was he was asking us to manage our risk," Daniel says. "The Chinese philosophy is, you cannot be greedy. If you get greedy, the risk will go up." For Daniel and his brother Richard, the challenge has been to remain true to a frugal attitude to risk without missing the timing for transformational acquisition.

the first six months for users to experience it firsthand. The product gained more than 100 million subscribers – a constituency that, were it to stand alone, would be one of the 20 most populous countries on Earth, bigger than Germany – within 170 days of launch. It is not unreasonable to argue, as Ambani does, that this venture represented the digitization of India, and that so many of the remarkable digital steps forward since then – the Aadhaar national identity card, for example, and the development of the largest open-source payments infrastructure in the world – rest on it.

In terms of finances the venture clearly delivered, and continues to do so: it has half a billion subscribers and is adding many more each month.[10]

So it's no longer really a question of whether the risk was worth taking. But how did Mukesh know that? Aided by a mighty balance sheet,[11] he had not only the money to chance capital but also the time to wait for it to pay off. This is an important characteristic of the way an Asian founder-entrepreneur thinks of risk: they can live with the fact that they might have to wait five years for a return in a way that a professional CEO, whose expected tenure might not be much more than that, cannot.

The Ambani story also tells us about another useful characteristic that comes with this extremely long-term horizon. This is the ability to break a daunting ambition into manageable pieces.

Let's say an ambitious new investment has a range of outcomes from a minus 10% return if it goes badly to a plus 40% if it goes well. The founder can break these 50 percentage points into smaller actions and bite them off and digest them one by one. Perhaps one is a renegotiation with a regulator, another the establishment of locked-in buyer. A third might be the need for a vital piece of supply chain infrastructure, perhaps a rail line, to be built in a certain time frame. Perhaps it's hedging, perhaps it's vendor negotiation, perhaps it's a technological advance, but whatever it is, the founder-entrepreneur will work through these achievable pieces consistently in pursuit of the grander goal, and in so doing, render risk manageable. Bit by bit, they convert worst cases to best cases. They make their own luck. And this takes time – the time that only a founder truly believes themselves to have.

The Rationale of Big Bets

When David Ku set up WeBank with companies including Tencent in 2015, he was trying something new: a digital bank making highly innovative use of social media and other data in order to advance the speed of credit decisions, with no physical branches and no use of property for guarantees. When Chinese Premier Li ceremoniously pressed a key in the company's Shenzhen office to initiate a CNY35,000 loan to a truck driver, it was the start of a unique proposition for Asia.

From the outset, Ku had choices to make about risk. "To me, risk appetite has something to do with what you want to do," Ku says. "The bigger your goal, the more you're willing to take risk."

That can look like conservatism or audacity, depending on whether Ku considers an opportunity to be worth the risk. He weighed the option of operating under a consumer finance license, which was relatively easy to obtain, but was uncertain about the regulatory certainty about doing what he wanted to do within the parameters of that license. Instead he waited longer to get a banking license, which was harder to win but offered greater clarity.

He was unwilling to take significant risk given the modest upside in the competitive consumer finance market, particularly if rules changed about what a consumer finance license allowed a holder to do. Waiting for a banking license, he said, "You will move slower. But at the same time, you're sort of safe." On this, he was right: after he made this decision, the Chinese government policy on the scope of consumer finance licenses changed. The more arduous, cautious path was the correct one from a risk perspective.

Murthy and the Risk of Walking Away

One of the biggest risks among our founder-entrepreneur group involved Infosys, and it was not the risk of a new business but of walking away from a key relationship.

In 1995, when Infosys was 13 years into its history and had been listed on stock exchanges for a year, one US customer accounted for at least 25% of its revenue – and it was turning tough. The US company, pitting multiple vendors against one another, sought to renegotiate its billing rates.

It did so with some aggression, and sequestered all its Indian software vendors into different rooms at the Taj Residency hotel in Bengaluru, so that they could not communicate with one other. The customer team would then go from room to room to seek the best terms out of each vendor and pit one against another for several rounds, pressuring each to accept unfavorable terms.

Narayana Murthy had previously sought to build a collective position among Indian software vendors to resist this bargaining ploy, but couldn't find common ground. Stuck and belittled in his hotel room, he had to make a call between harmful terms and walking away, with all the risk that decision would entail. And so he parted ways, an enormous step. His decision was shaped by a sense of justice.

"Fairness is my God," he says. "I did not see fairness in my transaction with that Fortune 10 corporation. When logic fails in any situation, you seek the realm of faith."

The decision had immediate practical consequences for him and indeed his family: he told his wife that giving up that business would commit him to spending 250–300 days a year traveling, staying in cheap motels, taking buses to destinations, and eating McDonald's to save money. His wife backed him completely, bringing up their children.

It worked. "I traveled like a possessed soul between June 1995 and June 1998," he says. "I ensured that our growth was much better than what we had planned even without that Fortune 10 customer's revenue."

But it did more than that. It pushed the company to think properly about risk, and brought about a rigor that remains to this day.

Until May 1995 Infosys had no risk mitigation group. The separation, along with a general sense that the company ought to evolve and professionalize, led to the development of a risk philosophy that became the Risk Mitigation Council. Part of its raison d'etre was that Infosys would never again depend too much on any one client, technology, country, or employee.

The team identified about 120 parameters of risk that could affect Infosys either directly or indirectly, measuring them at various periods of time from weeks to years. For the rest of his career, Murthy would employ these new approaches when considering opportunities. "In taking a decision, I ask for data which could bring huge benefits and which could jeopardize our future," he says. From then on, an outcome would be a matter of computation: of expected value, of scenarios, or probabilities. And that, rather than gut, would be his guide.

So from the pain of the loss of a key client stemmed a sound de-risking strategy that has stabilized Infosys's revenues, profits, and risk ever since. Modeling and simulations entered their strategy, while statistical and game theoretic models were developed and incorporated. And the result of all of that was younger colleagues who gained the confidence to try the outrageous, because they had learned to be prepared for the worst outcome while seeking the best.

"But if you ask me do I want to take a lot of risk on building a blockchain or [artificial intelligence] AI or digital assets business, my answer is yes," he says. That's because the potential value pool growth in consumer finance is relatively modest, he says. But digital assets could lead to half a trillion dollars[12] of value to capture, he believes. "My goal is I ought to capture 5–10% of that, and that thing is so big that I'm willing to take a lot of risk on it, as long as it is not something that can kill me." He's already started: WeBank has set up a technology company in Hong Kong to house new businesses for AI, blockchain, and digital assets.

Another example of a bold big bet – though one that is still too early to declare as a long-term success – is when Biocon's biosimilar arm, Biocon Biologics, acquired the biosimilar business of Viatris, a company formed by Mylan and Pfizer, for US$3.3 billion,[13] a record-breaking transaction for the sector in India at the time. Biocon had, Kiran Mazumdar-Shaw recalls, been offered a joint venture with Mylan, but preferred to take the bigger step and buy them out. "That was the biggest risk I took," she says.

Whether or not that deal achieves its potential, it is illustrative of a mindset that enables transformation in light of potential reward through the careful evaluation of risk. In 2007 Mazumdar-Shaw sold the enzymes business that had initially been the whole point of Biocon, and used that money to invest in biopharma, and then more specifically biosimilars.

She was guided partly by her overarching mission (in her case, a belief that India deserved world-class and affordable medicines) and considered the potential reward to be worth the risk she took. There was no recklessness. "I'm a big risk-taker, but it is a calculated risk that I take," she says. "I don't take absolutely wild risks and bet the whole business." She would not, for example, take on a big risk where she knew she did not have all the resources she would need to make it successful, she says. "I take risks where I know I have the resources, I have a mission, and then I take those risks."

Equally, and crucially, there are examples of Mazumdar-Shaw not taking that risk after a careful assessment of the potential rewards. She opted not to steer her business into novel molecules: the path was too arduous, it would take many years, and it would drain her resources, so it wasn't worth it. Her husband once described her approach to business as scientifically aggressive, but financially frugal; she has always had a cautious eye on the finances as she seeks to change India and the world.

These examples tell us the Asian founder-leaders have no fear of the grand, the transformational, and the expensive (or stepping away when something is wrong – see "Murthy and the Risk of Walking Away"). But they do so only if they believe that the level of risk is aligned with the potential reward. As many have said: taking no risk is the biggest risk of all.

Chapter Seven

I Move Forward if I Can Live with the Worst Case

"If a decision doesn't go our way, what would happen? Can we manage the worst case?"

—Sarath Ratanavadi, Gulf Development

"My assessment metric is this," says Dilip Shanghvi, founder of Sun Pharmaceuticals. "What is the worst-case scenario, and can I live with the worst-case outcome?"

This expression is echoed throughout the interviews in this book. Mukesh Ambani says, "When we say we will build something, we think about the worst-case scenario. We prepare for the worst, but we survive the worst because we know that even in the worst case, we won't lose everything." Joseph Tsai at Cathay says, "You cannot bet the bank. No, I wouldn't even get close to doing that." Sarath Ratanavadi at Gulf Development says, "We try to calculate risk and where we can take it. If that decision doesn't go our way, what would happen? Can we manage the worst case?"

Jeffrey Li of GL Capital is a long-standing admirer of Warren Buffett, and has applied many of Buffett's lessons to his own approach to private equity. "If you take leverage, 99% of the time, it will not affect you at all," Li says, recalling one such lesson. "But when you take leverage, what you should consider is the 1%. Is it going to kill you? Because if it is, don't do it. That 1% matters. The 99% doesn't matter."

It's important to note that, having assessed a worst-case scenario, founders do tend to have a strong stomach for it. Provided they know exactly how to quantify a risk, they have considerable tolerance. This helps us to understand that worst-case planning does not represent a negative mindset but a prudent one – and even being prudent doesn't mean they can't be audacious.

Risk as Freedom

Ho Hung Anh, the Chairman of Vietnam's Techcombank, puts it like this. "Identify for me a range or a space where I can be tolerant within it, and then I can act freely within that space." Risk management helps him to identify this space, which he achieves through nuanced stress tests and scenarios to assess resilience, "where if we invest in a new business and it fails and we lose all the money, it still doesn't hurt us too much."

"Once that is clear in our minds, we can act very freely without having to think twice within that space. But if I cannot control that space, especially when it comes to capital and liquidity, then I will be super cautious."

Ho's comments tell us that a proper assessment of the worst case represents not just prudence or caution but a freedom, a context within which risk may be taken without any existential fear. In Ho's case, he has had to pass up opportunity in order to stay within that clearly identified space. Earlier in his career he had been involved in setting up the real estate developer Masterise. The opportunity arose for Techcombank to acquire the developer and enter the real estate space, but at that time Masterise would have had to use Techcombank to raise funds, since it was not strong enough to do so independently. That, according to Ho's stress testing, wasn't going to work. "I always thought, should I enter real estate?" he recalls. "But I told myself no because it could have hurt Techcombank," since the bank wasn't strong enough to take on the funding backstop role for Masterise.

"Many people said, 'You are missing big opportunities.' But I did not regret it, because if I had gone down that path maybe Techcombank would not have been what it is today." And that is a 19% compound annual growth rate in pretax profit between 2018 and 2025[1] – a rate of growth made possible partly because Ho stuck to his convictions on worst-case scenarios, stayed out of an appealing business, and therefore had comfort to act decisively and aggressively in building the bank in a way that met his parameters for risk.

Dilip Shanghvi made his own calculations when deciding what to do about the drug Ilumya, which treats plaque psoriasis. Sun Pharma acquired the rights to the drug[2] from Merck in 2014 for an US$80 million up-front fee, a commitment to further milestone payments and royalties, and an estimated US$250–300 million in clinical development and trials through to FDA approval in 2018.

Shanghvi knew from the start what those costs were likely to look like – but, such are the uncertainties of FDA approval, he couldn't know definitively what those costs would be, nor the time frame. He balanced them against the opportunity for a new business and assessed whether he could live with that cost if the worst case happened and the product, for whatever reason, fared poorly. "I'm trying for the best case, but I'm prepared for the worst case," he says.

Risk Profits, Not Capital

When Dilip Shanghvi had identified his worst case, he worked out where the costs of addressing it would fall. "I will never risk capital. I will risk profit," he says. "The worst case is I may not make money that year, but I should not lose capital."

Shanghvi makes an important point here: one's ability to take risk at all is obviously bounded by one's capital position – balance sheet, indebtedness, the maturity of that debt, available credit lines. As Uday Kotak puts it, "Make sure you have more petrol than you need. Always have enough buffer of capital in case, God forbid, something goes wrong."

This is perhaps nowhere more true than in banking, where one only exists because of trust and the license of the state. More than that, increasingly onerous regulation for bank capital – devised for good reason following previous crashes and the loss of individual savings – brings about an extremely limited range for tolerable risk. As Aditya Puri, former Managing Director at HDFC Bank, puts it, "Banking is a fiduciary relationship. It's not my money. I've got to be 120% sure that I will never be in a position where anybody loses trust in me or I can't return the money, because that's the end of the bank. A bank *is* trust."

Uday Kotak explains it like this. If you start a bank with $10 of capital and borrow $90, you have $100. But you only need to lose $5 of your original $10 and you're out of business, as you're in breach of capital adequacy.

"With such a high-leverage business, you really need to be able to manage your risk and return very carefully," he says. "People forget: for the level of leverage, banks are among the riskiest institutions in the world, but are perceived to be the safest." As a banker, you would never lend to a business on a 10-to-1 leverage, he points out, yet it's exactly the same leverage you operate on yourself and consider acceptable.

Never Risk Your Reputation

Shanghvi and Kotak talked about the difference between risking profit and risking capital. But there is something else at the top of this hierarchy of the sacrosanct, something that cannot be risked in any circumstance: reputation.

There is a saying at Reliance: you can lose money many times, but you only lose respect once. This feeds into the company's overall risk metric. "If you lose your reputation, if you lose your dignity, it never comes back," Mukesh Ambani says.

This is easy to say but rather more difficult to effect in practice. What does it mean? Doesn't any potential failure have a reputational hit? At Macquarie, as a practical litmus test, they used to ask one another, "How would you feel if you saw this on the back pages of tomorrow's *Australian Financial Review*?" In the Reliance context, if Jio had gone horribly wrong, there would most certainly have been an impact on profitability for many years, and along with it a bigger hit on its reputation for executing massive projects and creating value. But regardless of commercial outcomes, Mukesh insists there is an insistence on doing what is right. "We will not embarrass anyone, and we will never do anything just for profit."

And, just like Macquarie wondering about the next day's front pages, this attitude bleeds through to a social context, too. "We wanted to ensure that if your children read about us, whether in business or in our personal lives, our values and morals would be such that we would never be embarrassed," he says. "You don't want your children to say: 'Dad, did you really do this?'"

Reputation matters far more than just a matter of personal conviction. It has practical, financial consequences, too. A loss of trust and reputation in a complex stakeholder ecosystem is very bad news indeed: if any one of regulators, government, shareholders, or board lose faith in management's reputation, there is a bigger problem than embarrassment. There is an existential threat because either money, permission, or license are at risk.

Chapter Eight

I Make My Own Luck

"I'm trying for the best case, but I'm prepared for the worst case."
—Dilip Shanghvi, Sun Pharma

There is a temptation to say that some of Asia's greatest success stories were in the right place at the right time.

That Techcombank rode the good fortune of being in Vietnam at the exact moment when national demographics supported a transformational swelling of everyday affluence; that WeBank benefited from a huge population comfortable with using only digital apps on smartphones, which was itself a consequence of China leapfrogging physical infrastructure as it developed; that Foxconn was founded just as Taiwan's export-oriented economy started taking off, enabling it to surf a wave of high-tech momentum.

Even David Ku says the performance of CEOs is "70% luck." Often surprisingly humble people, even founders themselves will often speak of their blessing of being in the right place at the right time.

Not so. Asian founder-entrepreneurs **make their own luck**, and the secret ingredient for doing so is their understanding of risk. Without the risk management underpinning the foundations of their businesses, all these challenges would have passed unmet.

Practices for Working Toward the Best Case

Founders understand that they can make their own luck through specific practices to increase their odds of success.

- **Bet on the right founders' team.** Founders surround themselves with a core, trusted team who embody the founder's DNA; they grow and work with these teams over many years.
  We can see this in the teams that Aditya Puri and Uday Kotak put together to build their banks, HDFC Bank and Kotak Mahindra, from scratch; also in Kaspi's Mikhail Lomtadze, who kept 80% of his product development team together over a period of almost 20 years.
- **Have a razor-sharp approach.** Another technique is what's known as the razor-sharp model, using a minimalist approach to building new businesses: "Spend your money on the blade's edge," *qián huā zài dāo kǒu shàng* (钱花在刀口上), as another Chinese saying has it.
  Good examples of this include Itaru Tanimura's development of M3, which launched extremely focused platforms at first, one doctor use

case at a time, and then built from there. Also in Japan, Akio Nitori's obsessive cost discipline across sourcing, logistics, and stores, expanding only when an operating model has become repeatable at low cost, recalls this approach.

- **Go all in.** An alternative to this minimalist approach is to throw the power of a whole enterprise at a challenge to give it the greatest possible chance of success.

  Mukesh Ambani is one of the best examples of this: the audacity of some of his ventures is balanced with the sheer scale of the resources he can put to the task. An endeavor as vast as Jio was only possible because of the amount of capital Reliance already had, with a robust balance sheet built on its success in the energy industry.
- **Learn from the best and adapt.** Asian founder-entrepreneurs have a long track record of studying the best practices around the world and adopting them (see also "Building for the Best Case Through Partnership").

  Jeffrey Li at GL Capital, for example, learned everything he knows about investment fundamentals from reading everything Warren Buffett and other successful investors ever wrote, then he applied it all to Chinese healthcare.
- **Have skin in the game.** Perhaps a final technique of making one's own luck is to go all in with skin in the game. We see this when Anand Mahindra puts the family name on every vehicle the company ever produces – and on Uday Kotak's bank, too. Founders put themselves on the line and they don't turn back.

Building for the Best Case Through Partnership

Bajaj Finserv represents a shrewd way of managing risk, and building towards the best case, through partnership.

Sanjiv Bajaj, who today runs Bajaj Finserv, came up through the finance function and along the way spent three and a half years running exports for the motorcycle business.[1] This taught him how to work with partners to build a network outside his home market, since in many jurisdictions – Sri Lanka, Bangladesh, Colombia, Mexico – Bajaj itself was unknown and the partner brand was everything.

He then applied these lessons as he built a financial services business "to be the financial life cycle partner to every Indian," he says. This was important because Bajaj wanted to build a bold network for the future, but would have undertaken a great deal of risk, and required a lot of capital and time, to do it organically.

Bajaj itself couldn't be a leader in every underlying field and product in a large, competitive market, so in addition to building its own products, Bajaj created an aggregation platform of other people's products that created the best and most convenient environment for customers. Bajaj Finserv Markets brings together 100 partners including banks, insurers, and mutual funds, while a digital health aggregator, Bajaj Finserv Health, links over 100,000 doctor clinics and 16,000 hospitals.[2] Bajaj Finserv has managed its ecosystem by being its ecosystem.

Sanjiv Bajaj achieved his goal without excessive risk because he knew how to partner.

Learning from Mistakes and Ring-Fencing Risk

A vital attribute in making one's own luck is the ability to learn from mistakes and to emerge from them strengthened, with something gained.

An institution that takes no risks is going to make no progress either. "Status quo is a killer of sustainable growth," says Saehong Hur at GS Caltex. "Accepting and embracing change means we take risks. But at the same time it is necessary."

That perspective has shaped what Hur describes as his *deep transformation journey*, which he set in motion in 2022. Hur believes organizations need a structural rather than an incremental model for transformation, where people across the company understand both the necessity and direction of change. To effect this, Hur speaks of a "black-box advantage," which refers to a set of deeply embedded and largely invisible strengths that are difficult for competitors to observe or replicate. These include unique processes and systems, organizational capabilities, and ways of working. As the transformation unfolds, this unseen competitiveness becomes a durable and differentiated source of advantage.

A useful discipline is to find a way to minimize the impact mistakes can have.

In the mid-2000s, as part of an effort to start serving India's vast rural population, HDFC Bank launched tractor financing. It went badly.

"Initially it was a disaster," says Puri, who was the bank's Managing Director from 1994 to 2020 – the longest such stint at any private sector bank in India. "When we would go to try to repossess the tractor, the farmer would say: this is my land. If you put a foot here, I'll chop it off." The product had been ill-thought out, and there were easier ways to make a return than to risk the loss of HDFC bankers' extremities. "So we pulled back and started all over again."

But the initial failure of this idea made not the slightest difference to the long-term fortunes of the bank. Puri had entered tractor finance as a pilot project, as he did with every other new idea. It was absolutely fine for things to go flamboyantly wrong, provided they did so within a contained environment in which the potential damage was clearly defined. "We were not risk averse," says Puri. "We made a lot of mistakes. But we found those mistakes in the pilot."

Better still, they learned from those mistakes, regrouped, and re-entered. Tractor leasing is now a mainstay product in rural banking, an extraordinarily powerful proposition in a country with a 1.4 billion population to serve, of whom 65% live in rural areas and 47% depend on agriculture for their livelihood.[3] Having made the mistakes when they didn't really matter, HDFC took what they had learned – that tractor leasing wouldn't work without the land as collateral – and applied it to build a successful product at scale. Consequently the mistake wasn't just survivable. It was important, necessary, in fact. It was a foundation for getting the product right. "Once we were clear this was a good idea, we ate like there was no tomorrow."

Puri's experience demonstrates the use of pilot initiatives as a method of protecting downside. In a pilot, one can try things out, understand mistakes, redesign, and then scale. "You innovate what you test," he says. "Fifty percent of our tests went wrong, and out of that 50, 25 we didn't do. The problem is the confusion between innovation and betting on that innovation. We never bet on an innovation without testing it out."

One of the most refined approaches to risk can be found at Australia's Macquarie Group. It has very clear common ground with Puri's position.

Over the years there have been a variety of internal slogans for Macquarie's approach, from *loose-tight* to *freedom within boundaries* to *failing to succeed,* but all reflect an ethos that has been in place ever since the top staff took the bank from being a Hill Samuel subsidiary to a free-standing institution called Macquarie Bank in 1984.

The essence of it is that Macquarie will back people with new ideas for businesses and give them considerable freedom to explore an unproven concept. But that's only half of the Macquarie compact. The other half is that in every single case, no matter how minute, Macquarie sizes exposures not only on the basis of whether the bank itself could survive a potential loss but also whether the individual businesses could do so. "When we looked at sizing risks, we sized them on the basis of the ongoing profitability and liquidity not just of bank itself but the individual businesses in the group," says Nicholas Moore, who joined Macquarie in 1986 and went on to be CEO from 2008 to 2018.[4] He speaks of the characteristics of a small business in a large organization.

There is a caveat to this: Macquarie is a heavily regulated institution and will instantly dismiss people who infringe any law or regulation, and it also expects their people not to engage in unacceptable sectors such as tobacco and deadly munitions. But beneath that, provided the Risk Management Group is happy with the risk-reward outlook, people have freedom to exercise their initiative and to make mistakes in the effort.

"If something goes wrong – and stuff goes wrong in business all the time – we had a very clear-eyed view about what we did. We owned up to it, we tried to put it right, and we always dealt honestly and with integrity."

Macquarie believes that sizing risk at the coal-face level – where the business is happening, not several management layers above it – is an act not only of trust but prudence. Moore remembers a predecessor saying that if something goes wrong in a business, "I don't want to be lying awake at night at four in the morning as chief executive, wondering what's going to happen. I want to know there's someone inside the business lying awake and owning the risk." To Moore, and to CEO Shemara Wikramanayake today, this spirit has not ebbed with Macquarie's increasing scale. "We wanted people who really wanted the power and the agency to say, 'This business is mine,'" says Moore. "I'm the person who's going to worry."

By and large, stakeholders – and particularly shareholders – can live with missteps if they can understand them. An error, appropriately disclosed and explained with transparency, is easily forgiven if it fits into an ethos that shareholders have already come to understand about an institution and the vision of its founder. But shareholders hate to feel misled, and they don't like sluggishness.

Learning from Mistakes at Foxconn

Sidney Lu at Foxconn recalls two distinct crises and learned from each of them. The first was in 1994 while developing CPU sockets for Intel. The connector itself worked fine, but it had a handle which, when closed, caused the whole device to fall apart. "That was a huge disaster," Lu recalls, but he learned from it. "The whole team panicked. I wasn't too pleased either. But I said, 'Calm down. Let's look at this.' It was actually a very simple engineering problem."

But what to do about it? He and his team worked for 48 hours straight to prototype a redesigned unit, which worked. "Two days. No sleep. Forty-eight hours." Then, they caught a plane, carrying samples of their new design, and went to Intel. "First thing we did was apologize. We said, 'We messed up.'" They demonstrated the new design worked right in front of Intel. And so they all moved forward.

"When you make a mistake, make sure you correct it fast," says Mazumdar-Shaw at Biocon – and her use of the word *when* rather than *if* is instructive, a recognition that mistakes will happen at any company built on entrepreneurial zest. "I know what it is to deal with setbacks, but you have to be resilient."

"It taught me to own up to our mistakes – and to resolve them."

Then in 2005 his team designed a memory socket with a swing design, which seemed to function fine at Foxconn's end, yet failed at Apple. This one could not be fixed – "this is the only product I designed in 43 years that didn't work" – but again the important point was what was learned from it. In this case, it was political: an enmity between software and hardware teams causing a failure to communicate. That was fixable, and in the meantime, Lu knew to own up and move on.

"The worst thing you can do with failure is to start looking at other people to blame, especially the people working for you, because then you don't earn respect," he says.

Reflective Questions

Bold but Bounded

1. Do you feel your portfolio of strategic initiatives reflects the right level of risk?
2. What is the worst case for you, and how are you managing your risks to avoid the worst case?
3. How are you making your own luck and executing toward your best case?

Innovate with Both a Big and a Small *I*

"Innovations need not be expensive, nor complex, nor high-tech. They just need to solve the problem in as easy and accessible a way as possible."

—Jaime Augusto Zóbel de Ayala, Ayala Group

Governing Mindsets

- **I'm obsessed with excellence.**
- **I look for opportunities to disrupt.**
- **I learn from the best, but adapt to make it my own.**
- **I want technology to solve a real business need.**

Narayana Murthy is known as an innovator on a transformational scale. "Innovation includes seeing opportunity in discontinuity," he says, and he built a career and a multinational out of it.

The whole Infosys story rests on innovation. Early on, Murthy matched the advent of relational databases on smaller computers in the United States with the supply of engineers in India. He then disrupted global information technology (IT) services by inventing and rolling out the global delivery model, which distributes IT services across a global network of onshore, near-shore, and offshore centers in a cost-efficient and risk-mitigated framework. Doing so allowed work to be done anywhere and pioneered new freedoms in the way business is conducted; it brought new ways to use spare capacity and specialist skills.

So Murthy will be remembered for this big-picture innovation. But he is very clear that innovation can also be a simple, incremental improvement in an apparently mundane process. "Infosys created a culture of constant improvement," he said. "Our focus on excellence started with every small thing we did."

That's an ethos he has spread throughout the company. Every Infosys employee is expected to ask themselves three fundamental questions each day:

- How do I do what I am doing faster tomorrow?
- How do I do what I am doing today cheaper tomorrow?
- How do I do what I am doing today with a better-quality tomorrow?

He says this culture of constant improvement starts at the most basic level of keeping toilets clean and turning up on time.

"Just big ideas alone will not result in betterment. It only happens if every employee buys into it . . . from the janitor to the executive chairman." Indeed, he once explained this methodology to a janitor, through the example of using a cloth in each hand to be faster, using cheaper products to be cheaper, and being fastidious in cleaning to create a better tomorrow.

"A mindset of constant improvement will only happen if we create an environment where everybody is doing it day after day," he says.

Murthy's attitude is a reminder that there is more than one kind of innovation. It's true that some innovations are dramatic, market-changing ideas: one might call this innovation with a big *I*. Big *I* innovation might be spotting a market failure and turning it into an opportunity, decisively and with commitment and scale. It might be a bold decision to grow by entering a new business. It might be bringing something completely new into the world, as Murthy did.

But the small *i* innovation – apparently minor things that are transformational in their own way – is just as important. Small *i* innovation is about the tiny improvement, the commitment to excellence, and the continuous effort to be better tomorrow than you were yesterday. Small *i* innovation is about the accumulation over time of small gains that stem from an attitude that one could always do more.

Innovation, to leading Asian founder-entrepreneurs, is as much about excellence and continuous improvement as it is about transformational technology. It is as much about simplicity and focus on the essential needs of the customer as it is about cleverness. And it is about finding market weaknesses and addressing them, on whatever scale that requires.

Chapter Nine

I'm Obsessed with Excellence

"I don't want to call them marginal improvements because any improvement is definitional."

—Michael Kim, MBK Partners

In the 1950s, Toyota began to implement a philosophy called *kaizen*. The word means "good change," or "improvement," and as a business method it means a series of small incremental changes over time that eventually amount to a significant positive impact. Popularized more widely in the 1980s by management consultant Masaaki Imai and engineer Taiichi Ohno, who developed the Toyota Production System, today it remains a management shorthand for achieving a big outcome from countless small steps.

Whether they call it *kaizen* or something different, the idea resonates with founder-entrepreneurs to this day. It requires a combination of operational excellence and a mindset of continuous improvement, so that progress is made from what is already a high starting point. This is what we might call the small *i* of innovation.

It is unsurprising to find it alive and well in Japan, where Akio Nitori has always applied it in his business. "Every year we aim to improve everything: denying the status quo, making products better from the moment they are created," he says. "Improvements are continuous and not emotional." Just like compound interest, an approach like this can yield considerable results over time: Nitori has long said that doubling or tripling an original goal can be achieved with perseverance.

"We constantly look for customer dissatisfaction or inconvenience, gather feedback from young employees for targeted products," he says. "Our company is large, but internally it still requires small, consistent improvement."

Michael Kim applies the *kaizen* methodology to the development of private equity. "For us, that's a philosophy, not a business practice or an organizational behavior tick," he says. Kim has come to understand that innovation can be an improvement within a much bigger process – in his case, buyouts – and that one doesn't have to reinvent the whole system to make it better. "The process of value creation is complicated in that there are a lot of moving parts," he says. "So if you can get just a couple of those parts improved, that for me is innovation."

Kim also pushes back against any temptation to call improvements small. "I don't want to call them marginal improvements because any improvement is definitional," he says.

While *kaizen* is known as a Japanese philosophy, its ethos has become widespread worldwide. At Sun Pharma in India, Dilip Shanghvi says his fundamental target is "to be better than last year" in each of his operating businesses. "So rather than competing with others, we try to better our own performance."

In Taiwan, where the attitude of continuous improvement is commonplace across the technology sector, Foxconn's Sidney Lu practices it daily.

"I'm constantly asking myself, 'Is this it? Is this it?' And the answer is always no. We can be better."

Small *i* innovation also includes a focus on cost: one clear area of potential for incremental gain is on the careful management of waste. Leading founders tend towards frugality, understanding that the largesse of transformational investment is afforded by a clear focus on costs, efficiency, and value. They don't tolerate lazy capital and they expect their money to work for them at all times. Founders are as good at identifying waste as they are backing bold ventures.

Innovate with Both a Big and a Small I opened with Narayana Murthy, and he exemplifies this belief. Murthy insists that every dollar Infosys spends serves a purpose to improve productivity, quality, or customer value. The attitude he brings to personal expense – living modestly for one so successful, eschewing extravagant displays of wealth – extends to his attitude to business expense.

One attitude that links to frugality is rethinking the industry to first principles: resetting to zero, as Akio Nitori puts it. This involves founders forcing themselves to step back from everything they think they know about the industry and reassess it from the absolute basics – and in particular, how a customer sees it. Nitori is a great believer in this resetting idea, re-examining retail, sourcing, logistics, and store design from the customer's viewpoint. This, once again, affords the opportunity for slight but continuous improvement.

Fang Hongbo does something similar at Midea, periodically stripping products and processes back to basics, removing features or even entire businesses that don't add clear customer value. "The goal," he says, "is to eliminate all activities that do not create value."

Chapter Ten

I Look for Opportunities to Disrupt

"What is your next wow factor?"

—Sidney Lu, Foxconn

What is big *I* innovation? It's about disruption. Sometimes it involves spotting an opportunity in the market by arbitraging imperfections. Sometimes it's grander, a moonshot: bringing something wholly new to the market. A large part of more transformational innovation – a whole new business or product – comes from the ability to spot a market failure and build something commercially successful to fix it.

What is a market failure? It isn't the same as spotting a long-term trend and building alongside it. In business it is defined as an outcome where the free market, with its customary balance of supply and demand, fails to allocate resources efficiently. In economics, it's a bad thing. To a founder, it's an opportunity.

Spot a market failure and address it, and you have a new business. Founders are very good at this. Kotak Mahindra exists because of what he calls "a very imperfect financial sector marketplace" in India, which invited the arrival of a sophisticated new bank with an ability to develop new products and business lines that the country lacked. Today, the bank he built to address this imperfection has a market capitalization of US$47 billion.[1]

Bajaj Finserv exists because the Indian market had failed to provide a comprehensive offering of products across the financial life cycles of individuals, from home loans to investment to insurance, with a minimum common standard of quality and transparency. That was a market failure. Bajaj fixed it and made a lot of money doing so.

Finding a market failure is a skill, and founders are very good at it. It can take many forms. Scan global markets to see what exists elsewhere that you might import at home (almost every founder in this book has done so, from Ayala applying international PPP models to water utilities in the Philippines to Joseph Tsai scouring the world for new investment products that might work in overbanked Taiwan). Study other industries to see what lessons can be brought across to one's own sector (such as banks like UOB and Bank Central Asia taking lessons from technology and rolling them into consumer banking applications). Look at gaps where a product should exist but doesn't, as M3 has consistently done in the provision of medical services in Japan.

M3's Itaru Tanimura thinks of innovation as problem-solving, which is its own way of addressing market failure. "People often say, 'Why didn't anyone do this before M3?'" he says. "The solutions we create often make people wonder why it wasn't done earlier." And pursuing this approach then translates into the bottom line: through it, M3 aims to keep its operating profit margin above 30% over the long term.[2]

Leveraging Capabilities to Enter Adjacent Businesses

One tactic for addressing market failure is adjacency: having filled one niche and gathered skills within it, looking around at something linked but distinct from it, and filling that niche, too.

One prominent example of this is Australia's Macquarie Group, which has used the adjacency principle ever since its earliest adventures in gold bullion in 1979. It started out as a broker offering two-way quotes, then began making a market for bullion as a principal, then launched futures. Within years it was hitting every possible angle of gold: buying, selling, supplying, delivering, storing, hedging, derivatives, and servicing every end of the chain. It worked for miners, investors, everyone in between, and made money from the volatility in the price at the same time.

Every step of this process involved spotting a gap – a market failure that they could only see because they had become adjacent to it, and had therefore accumulated the ability and the visibility to exploit that failure. They leveraged the competencies they already had. It's a particularly useful approach in a developing or maturing market where regulatory standards are still in flux and where new opportunities emerge.

By the 1990s Macquarie would go on to scale by changing its role in infrastructure from advisory to principal. In doing so it helped to pioneer infrastructure as an investable asset class, not just in Australia but all over the world. Nicholas Moore, the single biggest architect of this transition as he rose through the Macquarie ranks, recalls spotting the new potential asset category. "In building it up through adjacency, going off in all different directions, our role grew from an advisory to a company creator, an infrastructure fund and a developer, across all sorts of assets across the globe," he says. "Through adjacency, one little step at a time, we were able to grow it out." Macquarie is now the world's largest institutional player in infrastructure.

Takahara at Unicharm uses a form of this approach. He likes to start by digging deep into existing businesses to decide where it makes sense to innovate. By doing that, he says, "It reveals a world previously unseen and brings new ideas to light," an example being the menstrual and wellness management app, Sofy Be, which grew out of existing skill sets refined in another business. He calls it "a re-editing of strengths."

The Moonshot Approach

Another camp of big *I* innovation is the moonshot: the daring attempt to launch something new into an unsuspecting world that probably didn't know it needed it.

A moonshot is a first. It might not be a global first; many of our interviewees have taken bold steps to be the first in their country to do something and have been highly successful doing so. Reliance Industries has a long track record of moonshots across telecommunications, artificial intelligence (AI), and clean energy. Going further back, setting up India's first private sector refinery, or its exploration and production success in the deep waters of the Krishna Godavari Basin off India's east coast, were also moonshots, things that nobody had attempted before. Today Reliance Intelligence, its AI subsidiary, has been described as "India's moonshot to become an AI nation." Mukesh Ambani has approached these ventures with considerable dedication of resources, supported by the great strength of its balance sheet.

When Dilip Shanghvi founded Indian pharmaceutical manufacturer Sun Pharma, he sought to "create a product and business, a global multinational out of India. I believe there is an opportunity to create one." He wants an Indian company on the global stage with its own innovative products and the ability to market those products around the world. Sun Pharma is his moonshot, an India-based pharma company that sells in 100 countries. In fact, it's a moonshot idea that launches moonshot products when it develops new drugs aimed at US markets.

Probably nobody in Kazakhstan had any idea that what was missing from their life was a super app, but the evidence is that once it was built, people found they needed it (see "The Discipline of Innovation"). Mikhail Lomtadze built Kaspi's super app to beat Amazon at its own game, and several others besides: it brought together fintech, government services, a payments business, e-commerce, e-grocery, travel, classifieds, and other services. The result of this moonshot? The app has become so ubiquitous that it averages 15 million monthly active users in a country with a population of 20 million, all of them in turn averaging 77 transactions per month. About 70% of users visit daily, giving the app a higher level of engagement than Facebook, WhatsApp, or Instagram.

The Discipline of Innovation

Not every attempt at big *I* innovation is going to work, but at many founder-led companies there is a discipline to making oneself attempt the adventurous, with a tolerance for its potential failure. Murthy believes that every entrepreneur has the responsibility to innovate, not just the option. "I believe that the responsibility to innovate cannot be limited to any one function or a set of specialists in an institution," he says.

Others institutionalize a mentality that will encourage innovative thinking. Ayala, for example, has held at least 10 innovation summits in recent years, bringing in forward-looking speakers to inspire staff to think differently "and disrupt themselves meaningfully," Jaime Augusto Zóbel de Ayala says. Ayala is clear, though, that "there must be a very credible path to impact and scale in evaluating any innovation, and this is usually illustrated by strong proofs of concept early in the development phase."

Foxconn knows a bit about innovation, having used it as an engine to drive itself from a start-up launched with US$6,000 from Founder Terry Gou's mom's retirement fund to a company that reported US$260 billion of revenues in 2025.[3] Between 2000 and 2025, revenues grew 80 times over – equivalent to 20% compound annual growth rate over 25 years.[4]

Part of the reason for this extraordinary growth is a discipline to innovate. "What is your next wow factor?" Sidney Lu asks employees. "I say to people, 'This is what everybody will be expecting you to do. So what will you do differently?' That's what a wow factor is."

The need for this innovative attitude is amplified by the intense competition of the Taiwanese market, with so many excellent companies doing similar things in the chip industry. In such an environment, staying still is not only counterproductive but hazardous to a company's survival: they must always be developing the next thing, even when launching something else.

Growing up professionally in Hon Hai, Lu expected himself to come up with a wow innovation every three years. "That way you stay current and you stay young," he says. "You've got to have this refreshing cycle every three to four years, and well ahead of the three years you're already preparing," he says. "That's what gets you out of bed early."

Foxconn then permeated this attitude across the Taiwanese supply chain industries, and it is now commonplace.

Sometimes circumstances prompt a big *I* idea. Digital banking was already well underway by the time of the COVID-19 pandemic, but without question it accelerated the migration of consumers on to digital platforms they might otherwise have taken years to adopt. Given the extremes of the time, COVID became a practical proving ground for transformational ventures. M3 used it to dramatically advance technologies in mass telehealth and the logistics of vaccination across the country, particularly in rural areas.

The big *I* moonshot principle often requires a leap of faith – that it is worth entering businesses a founder doesn't yet understand in expectation that they will learn along the way.

Dilip Shanghvi of Sun Pharma has applied this principle to his work across the pharmaceuticals industry. "If I have a business in which we understand 70%, we are prepared to take the risk that we will learn 30% on the way," he says. He has done so when investing in specialty businesses, in which internally he might not know the specifics of market access, pricing, or restrictions when he starts. "We are comfortable with taking decisions where there will be a few things that we will solve on the way," he says. "We don't need to be 100% capable today."

Lomtadze at Kaspi uses the analogy of small children and their sense of fearlessness, something that often is eroded by the experience of adulthood. Put a small child on skis and they will probably figure it out because they have no trepidation. "Put me on the skis, I will not be a quick learner because I'm going to worry about breaking my leg." With this attitude, "entering a new business with very limited experience is also a competitive advantage," he says.

A Laser Focus on What the Customer Needs

When bringing about innovation, one thing is nonnegotiable for founder-entrepreneurs: an intense focus upon what the customer actually wants.

Customer Needs Through Simplification

Frequently a focus on customer needs results in a much simpler product than big *I* innovators might want to design. Simplification is the opposite of laziness: it takes great effort to simplify. Simplification brings a purity to the operation that benefits not only the consumer but also the enterprise.

We find a strong example of the drive for simplification in Kazakhstan, a distinctive market in Asia Pacific terms: vast in size, very low in population. Not blessed with the hundreds of millions of potential customers that he might find in India, China, or Vietnam, Mikhail Lomtadze sought to build a new kind of technology company, Kaspi, in a market of just 20 million people.

The small potential market made focus and innovation essential as he built his business. In high-population Indonesia,[5] a new player can make mistakes, have missteps, lose customers along the way because there are so many others to gain; not so in Kazakhstan, where every customer must be retained or the business won't be sustainable. "We couldn't do things which companies can afford in a market of 100 million people, where you can lose customers but still grow," says Lomtadze. "In a

What customers need is not necessarily the same thing as what innovation-minded companies want to give them. Founders recognize the correct way to organize this equation: find out what consumers need, then give it to them. Inventing some flashy new thing and then convincing customers they need it rarely works out (see "Customer Needs Through Simplification"). In this arrangement, customer-facing frontline staff are every bit as important as technology superstars.

"Customer is first, no matter what," says Akio Nitori. "Sleep, wake; it's all about the customer." Or as Ayala puts it, "We think that innovations should be based on solving pain points," with the proposed solutions being

20 million population market, if there are maybe 500,000 people who don't like your service, you are dead."

This pressure to get things right immediately has led Lomtadze to a technique. He calls it *extreme simplification*. Every potential product is pared back to what truly matters, then launched. Other features will be added over time, but at the start it will be pure in its focus. "It's very important that you launch something which is absolutely necessary and super simple," he says. In practice this meant speed, cost, and a better user experience, and once those were achieved, small *i* innovation became relevant, steadily refining and improving based on use and feedback.

Lomtadze has built an internal discipline in which staff must write a three-page explanation of a product in very simple language, answering questions such as: why will this product make customers' lives better? If that explanation requires complexity or assumption, the product is binned. "We say no a lot," he says. "We don't launch everything that comes to people's minds."

"You would be surprised how many companies are thinking 'we have all these people and they need to do something,'" Lomtadze says, "rather than asking what a customer needs."

scalable. "This people-centric, problem-focused approach ensures that innovations are relevant and meaningful and truly create value."

Achieving innovation in customer service requires a complete orientation toward that outcome. For example, rather than just tracking the usual metrics, Lomtadze thought hard about how his people were paid. He organized people on the product and did not give staff financial incentives, and certainly not key performance indicators related to financial metrics in the company. The only metric that mattered was the net promoter score (a customer loyalty metric) and customer feedback. In this way, the incentive becomes the quality of the service rather than the bottom line.

There's a central lesson in this: if you want to understand the customer, you'd better ask them directly what they want. Takahisa Takahara at Unicharm spends as much time as possible in stores so that he can learn about his customers. "I am conscious of getting primary information directly," he says. "I place great importance on contact with customers and try to make decisions based on actual reactions, not just figures."

Elsewhere in Japan, we see the same commitment to understanding the customer at Nitori.

Akio Nitori, now in his 80s, continues to try to find new ways of looking at things from a customer perspective, watching TV ads and checking products. "When I do that, problems just keep popping up," Nitori says, which creates the opportunity to innovate to solve them. People who don't see problems are problematic themselves, he says; they're not thinking about the customer.

Reorienting around the customer (see "An Obsessive Focus on the Customer Experience" and "A Continuous Revolution and Endless Renewal") is not straightforward and can take a lot of work if legacy systems have been oriented in a different way. As Joseph Tsai climbed the ranks of Cathay Financial he spent 10 years understanding different business lines, the asset portfolio, and in particular the 25,000-strong agent team who sold product. "The culture we had was very traditional, people-oriented and sales-oriented," he says. "The mindset of cultural change was to focus it more on the customer."

Doing so required some practical steps and a rethinking of established norms. For example, the Cathay Financial website was run by the information technology department. That made it technically capable but not attuned to client needs. "I've always felt if you take care of the customer – and take care of your employees – the numbers take care of themselves."

An Obsessive Focus on the Customer Experience

Sometimes an innovation isn't so much about a new technology or a smart new app as an aim for a quality of service. Jane Sun says Trip.com Group[6] "always tries very hard to exceed the customer's expectations." The company has technological expertise, for sure – it has 10,000 engineers – but it's service Sun keeps coming back to. She and her team track customer satisfaction and service outcomes closely.

She recalls a customer in Japan who checked in to a hotel to find it overbooked. He called Trip.com, and someone answered the phone in 30 seconds. Trip.com contacted the hotel staff and asked for his money to be refunded immediately. "There was a five-star hotel next to this four-star hotel. We made a reservation and gave it to him to stay for free." In cases of crisis – a tsunami in Japan, a crisis in the Middle East – this effort is redoubled, and within two minutes a team member is expected to reach out to customers in the region to ensure they are safe and fed, moving them if necessary. If they want to fly home, Trip.com commits to ensuring it happens the next day. And as company policy, if an issue is not caused by the customer, Trip.com will prioritize a refund even if the fault was with the vendor.

Sun's commitment to the customer was sorely tested during COVID-19. Nobody in this book was closer to the Ground Zero of the pandemic than a travel company: when the pandemic struck, hundreds of millions of people had their travel plans disrupted. The company made the decision to refund all customers, borrowing heavily from banks in order to do so, to the point that some questioned the company's ability to survive. It did, with its commitment to customers intact.

That might not sound like innovation, but if a level of customer service is greater than anything that previously existed in the industry, it most certainly is.

There Must Be No Sacred Cows

A key part of big *I* innovation is the willingness to cut a project, even an expensive or beloved one, if it isn't working. Founder-entrepreneurs understand there must be no sacred cows.

Many of our interviewees have taken painful steps in the pursuit of excellence. Fang Hongbo at Midea is one example. He says Midea is committed to embracing failure so that researchers are encouraged to explore new frontiers and ideas.

Fang only funds innovations that create clear user value at scale; if ideas add complexity without a proportionate benefit, he shuts them down. He speaks about having "the courage to subtract. This year,[7] we have reduced or exited businesses that are loss-making, unviable, or without future potential – those we once pursued with great ambition but that have proven beyond our capabilities," he says. "We simply cut them off."

"Innovation requires tolerance for failure," he says. "But it is equally important to stop losses in time." And that is not easy or intuitive. Knowing when to call it is a very difficult skill to master. It requires throwing away work that has required time and investment. "I often say the courage to admit defeat is more important than the courage to make mistakes," Fang says.

"We must not keep going further down the wrong path," Fang says. "We must have the courage to cut off a limb to save the body."

There are many other examples. Setijoso brought some very productive innovations and strategies to Bank Central Asia, but he also made mistakes, among them the Solitaire Lounge. The idea of this was to create a beautiful location for high-end customers, but it turned out people didn't have a plush lounge on their wish list, but rather good private bankers and products. BCA shifted its resources accordingly. Today Setijoso looks back at it as a lesson learned on "thinking you know what the customer wants without really analyzing what the customer actually wants." But he also knows that "the important thing is knowing when to cut losses."

Founders don't agonize about these things. They recognize that the price of innovation is occasional failure. What's important is what they take from the experience. Joseph Tsai at Cathay Financial speaks of also imparting this mindset onto his team. "It requires you to invest: let them make a mistake, or let us make a mistake," he says, "and then you move on and continue to learn from it."

A Continuous Revolution and Endless Renewal

Founders understand that part of a commitment to customer excellence is an acceptance that their work is never done, and that to believe otherwise is to invite inertia. But to establish what needs to be done next, it can be useful to go back to basics and to remind oneself of what people really need.

Anand Mahindra understood this, and set about a sequence of what he calls *yatras*: visits to often remote locations to meet customers and better understand their lives and motivations. It was frontier-spirited stuff: he would fly in a small turboprop and sometimes land in open fields, which on one occasion he couldn't disembark because an angry bull was in the way.

"I would choose a location – let's say Bihar – and then go to the tractor dealerships and meet customers of each of our businesses," Mahindra says. "The stories and personal energy that came out of those trips . . . . I should have been paying for the privilege of doing it."

It was all very colorful and energizing, but it had a bigger purpose too. "The key insight for me is that this is not a linear process with a beginning and an ending," he says. "The moment you finish something, you have to start doing a check again" – a check of what people on the ground want and need. "I saw it as a continuous process, a revolution, and by the time you've finished one cycle, you may have to start looking at it again to see if you need to tweak your vision. That cycle is never-ending."

Chapter Eleven

I Learn from the Best, but Adapt to Make It My Own

"You in me, and me in you."

—Fang Hongbo, Midea Group

Asian companies are disrupting the price-value equation. Whether it's China's continuous innovation in electric vehicles, bringing prices down to a point that international competitors like Tesla can't reach, or India in med-tech, there is an obsessive desire to produce steadily better specifications for lower cost and at greater speed.

Asia has reached a leadership position in disruptive innovation partly by knowing how to adapt ideas from elsewhere. Throughout the 1980s, 1990s, and 2000s Asian countries – and China in particular – would learn from the best in the West and then bring expertise or technology home to roll it out in their own unique way. Sometimes these meant organically incorporating new ideas, sometimes it meant acquiring strong Western companies and reverse engineering their technology.

For example, between 2015 and 2017, Midea acquired Kuka, the German industrial robotics company. Kuka was a symbol of German engineering excellence and its Industry 4.0 capability,[1] and is considered one of the world's leading robot manufacturers. Leveraging this ability, Midea set up a factory in 2020 that has since delivered more than 80,000 industrial robots. It has now developed its own research and development strength in robots, and in March 2025 showed a prototype that can perform handshakes, dance, open bottle caps, and drive in screws.[2]

At GS Caltex, Saehong Hur freely states that "we are using external technologies to make innovation happen within ourselves." Much of this has involved partnership across lower-carbon growth businesses including biofuels – collaborating with airlines and shipping companies to demonstrate sustainable fuels and supply them commercially. Sometimes GS Caltex has pursued selective acquisitions such as equity stakes in startups of recycled plastics businesses. Alongside these efforts, GS Group works with CVC to develop corporate venture capital funds to look at companies with emerging technologies that might be acquired in order to help GS Caltex's expertise.

But Hur recognizes that learning from others isn't a complete fix. "If we work with outside vendors, yes, we can create a fancy solution today, but down the road when the market changes and there are new tools, we will have to hire them again," he says. "That's not a sustainable way. We thought: we have to build an internalized capability." This is expressed partly through a platform called DAX Center, combining digital and AI capabilities, which includes re-skilling existing petrochemical and refining engineers in new areas to encourage diversification of the company's portfolio. "It comes from an experimental mindset," he says. "Let's do it. If it fails, fail fast and learn from our mistakes and let's do it again."

A similar pattern can be seen at CP Group, the Thai conglomerate. Suphachai Chearavanont recalls his father revolutionizing chicken and swine farming in Thailand. At the time, people raised 200 chickens at most on small household farms. "In the US and Europe, they raise 10,000 or 20,000 livestock," Suphachai's father told him. "If they can do it, we can do it."

"So he traveled, learned the processes and technology, and brought it back to Thailand," Suphachai says. Today, CP Group raises three million chickens. "But it wasn't easy. There were many failures. It took almost 15 years to perfect large-scale chicken farming."

Much like GS Caltex, CP Group has built a Center of Excellence to conduct research and build new capabilities while quickly responding to new technologies. Thus a company that once went to America to learn how to do things has invested in the capability to learn how to do it unassisted.

This attitude brings us to the idea of leapfrogging. Having learned from others, frequently Asian companies jump right past an existing norm to establish a new one (see "Reinventing Asian Capitalism at MBK"). Digitalization has enabled many Asian countries to bypass older infrastructure common in the West and move straight to more efficient and digitally native systems. Digital payments is perhaps the clearest example, and many of our interviewees – David Ku at WeBank, Mikhail Lomtadze at Kaspi – illustrate the trend, moving straight to digital-only banking systems (WeBank) or mobile payments (Kaspi). The high-speed rollout of 5G in markets like India and China (notably by Reliance Jio) is another example. Today India is one of the world's most densely covered 5G data market.

Reinventing Asian Capitalism at MBK

Michael Kim's strategy at MBK Partners illustrates the principle of taking an idea and making it distinct to Asia.

When Kim set up South Korea–based private equity (PE) firm MBK in 2005, his mission was in some sense blunt. "Our North Star is simply to be the best PE firm in Asia," he says, leading with the highest standards. "It's a simple vision." But behind that was something more precise. "Our mission, which we articulated 20 years ago, was to be an agent of change in our North Asian societies," he says.

The method of Kim's agency was quite specific: introducing alternative assets as a real asset class in Asia, which he believed had a role to play in developing a sophisticated financial market. Developing the asset allocation structure in Asia then has further knock-on effects, all the way from sovereign investment to the savings of retirees.

This is a classic example of learning from the best and adapting. Kim brought a commitment to localizing, partly in terms of whom he hired, but particularly a local way of doing things, borrowing Western practices and giving them an Asian twist.

In particular, he looked at leveraged buyouts. These can be controversial – Kim was himself subject to criticism in South Korea's parliament over his firm's buyout of the Korean hypermarket chain Homeplus – but he believes the availability of these structures was important. "That was a technology that Asia needed," he says, but it had to be adapted to local standards and circumstances. "You have to basically Asia-ize the product."

So when he says "I consider myself an agent of diffusion in Asia for private equity," he is taking a sophisticated technical method to achieve something considerably bigger: finding a new form of Asian capitalism, one that embodies Confucian values of social respect and group harmony, for the benefit of Asia.

Chapter Twelve

I Want Technology to Solve a Real Business Need

"We use external technologies to make innovation happen within ourselves."

—Saehong Hur, GS Caltex

It is easy to throw a lot of money at technology and digital disruption without necessarily thinking through where the return is going to come from. The best founder-entrepreneurs are willing to advance spending on innovation, but not without a clear idea of where it will get them. They don't want technology for technology's sake; it must deliver an outcome. That might be an enablement to do something they couldn't do before, or an existing process with greater efficiency, or it might be as an agent of disruption in order to exploit a new opportunity. But it has to do something.

Aditya Puri at India's HDFC Bank has long had a reputation for heavy investment in technology (to the entertainment of his staff, since he almost never used a mobile phone).

But Puri always insisted that he be guided accurately on the return on investment that would follow. "You shouldn't just define why you're going into cloud," he says by way of example. "You should monitor whether you're achieving it, then see if you've got the right amount of capacity or if you're paying too much." In everything he touched, he insisted on the same process of monitoring and verification. "So when you say you're going for digital marketing, unless you have proper analysis of your data on the customer to be able to give them a hyper-personalized product backed by the right campaign, it's going to be a shotgun," powerful but unfocused. "If you keep to purpose, it's going to be a rifle shot," far more precise. "And then you must keep improving on it."

In the spirit of this precision, he would offer great independence and backing to his technology staff – but with a clearly expressed bargain in mind. "I said, not only will I give you leeway, I'll let you have whatever you want," he says. "But let's be very clear up front: you will tell me what I get at the end."

Puri always insisted on making sure that technology, marketing, and finance people all knew what they were talking about and worked together, enabling proper monitoring. And it's notable he doesn't boast about being first to a particular technology, but a particular outcome. "We were the first to offer anywhere, anytime banking, because we had distributed services and centralized processing." Note the order of that statement: outcome first, enabling technology second.

Takahara at Unicharm takes this a step further when he says that data, in its own end, is not enough. "We often talk about being data-centric, but market data only shows one aspect of behavior," he says. It doesn't show the causes, and without that, it's not enough to develop a product. So by all means collect data in real time, he says, but "it is more valuable to spend more money on investigating the roots that led to the phenomenon."

This is not to suggest that founders aren't prepared to take a bold step in a technological advance if they feel the time is right: they have great conviction in everything they do, and technological disruption is no different. But that conviction will always be married with an expectation of a return.

Technology is a Means to an End

Puri and HDFC Bank are also interesting in what they use technology for. It is never sufficient to just have the best tech. It has to take you somewhere. He says, "Technology is an enabler for you to develop services, not an end in itself."

Puri was only able to pilot the bank toward the untapped opportunity of underbanked rural India because a step change in technology permitted him to do so. "We were the first ones to say we were going into the interior country, because technology now allowed us to go for less populated areas," he says. "Technologies allowed us to do the credit assessment, the payment, the collection."

Wee Ee Cheong at UOB is another who believes technology must act in service of a client need, rather than being an innovation in its own right. "We are not a technology company," he says. "We are a bank."

He is prepared to eschew leadership in technology (UOB's neighbor DBS Bank is a notable pioneer in technology). "I don't need to be the first one," he says. "I can be a fast follower."

Similarly, Ayala Group is explicit in its insistence that technology isn't the point of innovation. "For us, innovation has a purpose: it should create value, or else it's merely new invention that can easily be discarded when disrupted by new technologies or a novel business model," says Jaime Augusto Zóbel de Ayala. "This is usually the case in the development of new technologies – that it can mostly be like a solution looking for a problem, which can be quite expensive, while being unsuccessful in resolving problems."

Jane Sun says Trip.com Group considers itself "a travel company heavily empowered by technology – if we just stayed as a traditional travel company, we wouldn't have done so well."

For example, there is a requirement that anywhere in the world, a live person must answer a call in the caller's native language within 30 seconds. Artificial intelligence (AI) is used to help this happen – and its TripGenie AI tool solves about 75% of routine queries. The company has 10,000 engineers working not only to innovate products but to enhance the customer experience.

Trip.com's use of AI recognizes that there are generational differences in how people want to be treated. "The end result is not an automatic ratio," she says. In some cases, like standard inquiries or in queries from younger people, AI is better, she says. "Young people don't like to talk to people if there is no issue." But if there is an issue, a human is needed. AI is only useful if it solves a problem for the consumer. "The end result is make sure your customer is happy. That's the focus."

Where Technology Transforms

For some businesses, however, technology really is transformational. "We don't do anything without leveraging the internet or technology because it wouldn't differentiate us," says Itaru Tanimura at M3. In fact, M3 was just an internet company between 2000 and 2010, without any operational infrastructure, but it hit a ceiling in what it could achieve so it began building operational capability, somewhat to the chagrin of investors at the time.

These operational initiatives then brought M3's product closer to real-world applications. The first was supporting doctors with career transitions. There was a job site for doctors, with revenue earned from hospitals and agents advertising on it, but the quality of agents varied, prompting M3 to handle operations itself; now, when a doctor applies, 80% receive a call within a minute.

Today, the medical business uses AI to address wastage, such as digitization of medical records, and by reallocating resources from unnecessary treatments to necessary ones. Using the example of hypertension medication, he suggests this can lead to an 80% reduction in medical expenses. "AI can identify these patterns, even if we don't fully understand why."

Technology helps M3 achieve its original vision. Even as technology evolves, the goal remains to increase the number of people living healthy and enjoyable lives while reducing unnecessary medical costs. He says M3 is working on 40 themes across 20 countries to address 1,600 potential areas, and so far has only tackled about 5%.

M3, then, is a good example of a company that uses technology as a disrupter and an enabler. It has enabled doctors' daily work through efficient digital platforms, and at the same time it has disrupted pharma marketing and clinical research models from end to end.

We should expect all the founders in this book to make insightful use of AI, and many are already doing so (see "Midea's Digital Intelligence Investment"). These founders are obsessed with finding ways to create value from technology, be it productivity gains or building new businesses. Just as they don't use technology for its own sake, they will expect AI – and the investment in it – to pay off in practical, positive outcomes.

Midea's Digital Intelligence Investment

Midea is another company for which technological innovation is key. Fang Hongbo says that launching Midea's digital intelligence transformation was vital "because I realized that this transformation was not an option but a necessity for Midea," he says. He saw it as a foundation to improve efficiency, and also the cornerstone to achieve his vision to take the company from a traditional Industrial 2.0 manufacturing enterprise to a modern technology-driven company powered by innovation, technology, and big data.

When a founder is convinced a technological advance must be made, they know it's going to cost. Fang's Digitalization 1.0 Project – also known internally as the 632 Project – covered six systems, three management platforms, and two technology platforms, attempting to overcome a decentralized internal structure to bring the whole company to one system and standard. The implementation of this project consumed one third of annual profits during its inception and took three years to unify processes, data, and systems.

A second project, Digitalization 2.0, followed in 2016 and introduced big data, mobility, and intelligent manufacturing. This era brought what Midea calls *industrial internet*, building the Midea M.IoT integrated Internet of Things platform with a pilot in Midea's air conditioner factory in Guangzhou. A third, Digitalization 3.0, started in 2023 and deepened a direct-to consumer digital ecosystem strategy.

That pilot shows how the effort of transformational innovation can be rewarded. Manufacturing efficiency improved 44%, monthly production capacity doubled, and the factory achieved a "dark factory" model, operated primarily through autonomous machines. Through it, the domestic air conditioner delivery cycle was shortened to as little as three days. Subsequent digital initiatives, particularly through the pandemic, have also had transformational impact.[1]

Reflective Questions

Innovate with Both a Big and a Small *I*

1. Small *i*: How are you mandating and empowering your organization to do things better, faster, and cheaper than last year?
2. Big *I*: What disruption are you catalyzing? How are you capitalizing on the biggest industry discontinuities shaping your business?
3. How do you ensure technology generates a return on investment and serves a true customer need?

Derive Extraordinary Outcomes from Talent

"Our hires did not have the reputation for being extraordinary. They had the confidence to be extraordinary, and they needed a canvas."

—Aditya Puri, HDFC Bank

Governing Mindsets

- **I recruit for character and fit.**
- **I develop people through stretch opportunities.**
- **I take a through-cycle approach to people.**

Dilip Shanghvi uses a distinctive analogy to explain how he assesses the contribution of his employees. "There are companies which have only a current account," says the Executive Chairman of Sun Pharma. "We have both a current and a savings account."

What does he mean by this? That long-term efforts for the company, even if far in the past, should not be ignored if an employee is struggling today. Their historic contribution – their money in the savings account, in his analogy – will be remembered. "If an employee is not doing great in the current role, but did remarkable things in previous roles, I personally would give a value to what that person did back then," he says. "Before I ask people for loyalty, I am prepared to be loyal to them."

Shanghvi's position is part decency, part pragmatism. He understands that just as he may go through highs and lows, so too may his employees, and they ought to be assessed on the aggregate of their work rather than at a difficult moment. "I have made many mistakes in life," he says. "I don't want to use a standard which is different for myself and others."

But he also knows that his own loyalty will be rewarded in the cohesion of the team that operates and grows his business every day in alignment with his vision.

Asia's leading founder-entrepreneurs are, like Shanghvi, bonded by some distinctive and often contrarian attitudes toward their workforce. From recruitment to development, retention to succession, they have striking common ground.

They prefer to mold their own talent through internal development rather than bringing in those with deep professional experience at another company. They give opportunities to people and take risks on them, moving them around beyond the defined scope of their role so that they can develop. The founder role here is in leadership and strength of character, providing a psychological safety net and serving as problem-solving mentors.

Their approach is at odds with what one is taught in Western management schools about managing people: hire the best, give them clear roles with strong rewards and recognition, hold them accountable, and fire them if they underperform. In Asia, these norms are inverted: hire inexperience and mold them, give them roles with the ability to stretch, be tolerant with mistakes, and keep the ones who perform as part of the corporate family for the long term. Many of these ideas, which were instinctive to founders, are now being copied elsewhere.

The approach is not absolute. For professionals hired from outside for specific purposes there may not be quite the same largesse: founders can be as ruthless as Western CEOs in letting these people go if key performance indicators are not met. But in a founder's inner circle, and for those who have grown up within a company's culture, it holds true.

At the heart of this Asian philosophy is a central idea: founders seek to get the extraordinary from their people. And when they do, like Shanghvi, they treat these people like extended family, understanding and gaining from the fact that talent will develop and grow over the very long term if they are given the right environment within which to flourish.

Chapter Thirteen

I Recruit for Character and Fit

"You don't just need a few stars."

—Ho Hung Anh, Techcombank

One of the most widely shared characteristics of founder-entrepreneurs in Asia is the belief in developing people from within rather than relying on external hiring. Many founders prefer to take unproven and often young or inexperienced talent and to mold that talent into what they need. Hiring established stars from rivals has its place – and at certain stages of development many companies will need to both hire people and develop existing staff – but is far less prevalent among founders as a strategy for development than it is for professional CEOs.

The preference for internal development over external hiring is partly a necessity of Asia's environment. Asia has long had a talent crunch, as rates of growth in Asia Pacific companies often exceed the pace of education and experience to support that growth. Education and training systems across Asia are varied and gradually maturing, but as they do so, this talent crunch – the mismatch between the skills of the region's workforce and the skills their employers need – is a problem for companies seeking to hire the right people.

On top of that, there is a predisposition not to make people redundant, which is far more entrenched in Asia than in Europe and, in particular, the United States. There is an unspoken social contract commonplace in Asia that when one joins a company, one stays there (sometimes a double-edged sword). Upskilling is more important than replacement. And if skilled people don't leave one place, they can't be hired by another.

Given this talent bottleneck, enterprising companies find it prudent to try to grow their own timber from within. Where Western companies might simply hire what they need, in Asia, the core of any workforce is upskilling and re-skilling the people who are already there.

So part of the reason Asian founders prefer to grow from within is because they have to. "It's all a function of necessity," says Dilip Shanghvi. "When I started the business, because we were not a known company, we had no great financial resources, so we had to hire people we could afford. And because the business demanded that we continue to grow rapidly, the only way by which we could deliver was by having these people deliver far beyond their capacity. And I think we did that quite well."

The Benefits of Building from within

While growing one's own timber is partly a necessity of circumstance, it's also a preference: Asia's best founder-entrepreneurs like the idea of the blank sheet of paper to work on. They would rather not seek ego-driven star players, but instead build with people who may lack experience but bring a strong work ethic and a willingness to learn.

Many leading founders have experienced disappointment when they brought in proven expertise. When David Ku started to build WeBank he sought to put the best talent together by hiring, "but soon you realize that these people have their own agenda." He made some early hires who appeared excellent; several left swiftly after internal disputes.

"We started to realize that you don't necessarily need the best talent, but having what you have and then having them work together is more important," he says. Building on that basis enables one to form a coherent common vision. "You have to align all these people on how you see the world." Ku's discovery was that it was only possible to build such a unified vision by seeking people earlier in their career who could be molded, rather than those who had already set upon a method of working with another employer.

Ho Hung Anh went through the same learning process when he joined Techcombank in Vietnam in 2008. There was some talent there, but not sufficient for market expectation as the Vietnamese economy boomed. So he had two choices: find experienced stars and pay them big money to join or build homegrown talent.

The big money approach is not without merit, he says. "It's not a bad approach because it allows for very fast evolution and growth, but if we want to build a sustainable foundation we need to rely more on long-term corporate culture that is more binding and cohesive." That means eschewing the star for the greater good, working with people who understand the corporate culture and developing them over time. "With banking and financial services, if you want stability you need a critical mass," he says. "You don't just need a few stars. So I chose to focus on the existing talents I had with coaching and training."

Choosing this option, Ho can say from experience, means a long commitment to hard work in development. But it is worth it. "In theory, talent development is the same everywhere, but what is important is whether you choose to go short term or long term. I've decided to choose the harder way, which is the long-term way," he says.

Kiran Mazumdar-Shaw has reached similar conclusions in her almost 50 years of building Biocon. From the outset of the business in the late 1970s, the parameters she set for her people were much more about open-mindedness than experience. "It's easier to develop people when they come fresh from universities and shape their minds rather than to try to take very experienced talent from the same sector or industry, because they come with a mindset, an attitude," she says. "People come from universities with an open mind. You don't want people who are brilliant but not interested in anything else."

When she looks at Biocon today, with its 20,000 headcount, of whom 70% are scientists and engineers, she finds that most of the experts have gained that expertise alongside her: they have grown with the company over 25 or 30 years. "I think Biocon is a living example of getting ordinary people to do extraordinary things."

Recruiting for Character Over Expertise

When it comes to hiring, founders value character more than evidence of existing competency, because they believe they can develop that competency within the company. If they fill their workforce with people they believe to have the correct character, it will be much easier to seek alignment with the founder's corporate culture.

A clear articulation of this distinction comes from Reliance Industries second-generation leader Mukesh Ambani. "We hire owner-operators, not professionals," he says.

What's the difference? "A professional will give you a rationale of why this did not happen, and take credit for whatever did happen." Ambani would much rather be dealing with someone who feels like they live and breathe the business. "An owner-operator will come with bruises," he says. "Even if they fail, they will say: give me one more chance and I will succeed the next time. That is . . . the person I will bet on every time."

Mukesh is defining character here, and his view goes all the way back to his father Dhirubhai's foundation of Reliance. "My father was clear: these people weren't just employees, they were cofounders," he says of the original team that built Reliance. In the first 20 years of the company's existence, those team members often had roles more significant than the founder himself, Mukesh says.

How Founders Hire with Culture in Mind

When founders hire for character, they need to be clear on what that means. For some, it is a symmetry with an existing corporate conviction. "The primary factor that we look for is a strong alignment of the talent with Ayala's purpose and values," says Jaime Augusto Zóbel de Ayala at Ayala Group. "We want talents who believe in the mission of the company," such as sustainability, stewardship and long-term investing. "There may be tremendously talented individuals out there, but all these would be for naught if the right values and attitude are absent."

"The individual would simply not survive in Ayala's culture if the person is not aligned with the company."

When Falguni Nayar founded Nykaa, "I used to joke that trespassers will be recruited," she says. "So if someone had passion for our vision and goals, we should just have them on board." Back then, this passion was more important than experience, though obviously as the company has grown to more than 4,000 employees, hiring priorities have shifted to getting the right skill sets for different roles. Still, vision is at the heart of Nykaa's culture, and to make sure people understand it, she runs business planning sessions with as many as 200 people. That creates a risk of crucial business information leaking, but she is willing to take that risk to afford her people the opportunity to learn directly from her.

Falguni recognizes the importance of a company being able to convey what its culture is, and to find people who align with it. For this reason, to achieve the best hiring outcomes, many founders have historically involved themselves in the front line of recruitment at the top tier of corporate hiring, and some still do.

Takahisa Takahara, President and CEO of Unicharm, says he is directly involved in all final interviews, and says they "are not ceremonial. It is an opportunity to determine whether the person is really needed by the company." And to make that determination, he is looking fundamentally at character.

Questions in a Unicharm interview seek, more than anything else, to uncover a candidate's motivation. "We dig deep into the roots and ask questions to find out the essence of their motivation for applying for the job."

Elsewhere in Japan, M3 Founder Itaru Tanimura personally conducted all final interviews until 2024. "Investing an hour in hiring the right person is more efficient than hiring the wrong person and dealing with the problems they cause later," he says. He reviews all internal recruitment videos (albeit at 2.5 times speed) to decide whether to approve candidates.

He thinks this seniority in hiring is important, citing a Microsoft truism that A-level talent hires people better than themselves, but B-level talent won't because they will see the potential employee as a threat. B-level talent, therefore, hires C-level talent. "Before you know it you're down to Z-level talent," he says. "That's why we focus on opening the door for A-level talent." He prides himself on identifying people without polished profiles but with great potential.

Many see interviews as a two-way street. Daniel Tsai at Fubon personally interviews recruits and management trainees, sometimes packing five straight days with 10-minute interviews. "It's not just about you trying to get to know the person, but to let the interviewee get to know you," he says. "I want people to hear firsthand from me what my hopes for them are, what our goals are for the company. I want to synchronize our thoughts."

Anand Mahindra is closely involved in senior recruitment, insisting on a 90-minute conversation with anyone who is joining at the top. These conversations are deliberately unstructured: "Let's just see where it goes." He asks candidates to talk about themselves, what drives them. He asks about them growing up. "People are shaped by their upbringing. If you don't ask a person about his family, you'll never get to know about them."

Again, what Mahindra is looking for here is some illustration of character. He recalls a salt-of-the-earth person who came to join them in the farm business. "He said to me 'Anand, if I come to work for you, I will not be working for you. I will be working for the people who work for me.' I was blown away. This person made people do extraordinary things."

Practical Methods of Hiring for Character

Naturally, founders can't involve themselves directly in interviews too far down their organization: they don't have time. So further down, other techniques must be used.

Nitori receives 150,000 applications from graduates each year, and screens this number down to 10,000 with tests.

And returning to Ayala, Jaime's grand statements about alignment with vision are tightly incorporated into human resources (HR) processes, functioning as a lens for recruitment; the onboarding process incorporates modules on the history of Ayala so that people join with a sense of history and responsibility. Values are used in performance evaluation.

It's interesting how hiring for reasons other than technical capability can lead to some distinctive outcomes. Michael Kim at MBK knows plenty about the importance of culture as an alumnus of Goldman Sachs. He also knows he faces a particular challenge when he seeks to hire for cultural unity, given that MBK operates across Japanese, Korean, and Chinese cultures, yet must find a way for all of these teams to work together.

While Kim has practical techniques for getting people to work together – a huge emphasis on training, standardized ways to write memos and approach due diligence, and "more bonding than probably any other organization" – one of the key elements is what he looks for in hiring. Kim favors high-IQ people with liberal arts backgrounds, believe that such people are better able to make connections between previously unconnected things, a skill that requires a broad base of knowledge.

"We hire people [who] are a little bit different," he says. "We can teach people how to do diligence, how to analyze, how to run financial models, but we can't teach them how to think."

It's intriguing that Mahindra & Mahindra, too, tends to look for people with liberal arts backgrounds, which is not common in big business. When Anand set up the Mahindra Universe Program with Harvard Business School, he insisted on a curriculum with an equal split between business case studies and the arts.

The Importance of Placing Talent Correctly

Once hired, it is vital that talent be placed in the correct place – though founders consider it important that they have the ability to change their role over time. "If you give the wrong job to an incredible person, they will not be able to perform," says Mikhail Lomtadze, founder of Kaspi in Kazakhstan. That's chiefly an HR challenge, but founders are notable for the pride they take in their intuition to spot the correct place for a talent.

That requires a recognition, both at the level of the individual employee and the team leader who must get them to work together, about the practical realities of what people can do. "We should be very tolerant of the differences" in people and their skills, and recognize these differences in attempting to build teams, says Jane Sun at Trip.com Group. "As a leader I always tell my direct reports it's very important for them to realize what they're good at, what they're not good at, and to be humble enough," she says.

"The worst is if you're good at one thing but you think you're good at everything and think your teammates cannot help you out. That would be very dangerous."

Sarath Ratanavadi at Gulf Development has a similar attitude: trust employees as you develop their strengths. "Never blame, and recognize that everyone has unique strengths," he says.

Chapter Fourteen

I Develop People Through Stretch Opportunities

"If the work is meaningful, you're going to grow."

—Joseph Tsai, Cathay Financial

When Anand Mahindra was at university, a professor told him that boxes don't define people, people define the box. They expand it or contract it depending on who they are. He took the advice to heart and has applied it ever since.

In Western management literature it is common to have clarity in a role about both what it entails and what it specifically does not. Asian founders sometimes enjoy the fact that roles in their organizations can be deliberately more opaque in their definition because that allows for the flexibility to stretch people and for them to address new challenges as they arise. Doing so also avoids the danger of isolated silos developing within a business.

Mahindra cites a remarkable example of moving an employee far beyond their defined role. Veejay Nakra is today President of the Automotive Division of Mahindra & Mahindra, but he started out much lower: the "EA [executive assistant] to my EA," as Anand puts it. But back then, Mahindra looked to Veejay when there was a need for someone to represent a business in South Africa.

"Everyone thought it was nuts," Mahindra says. "I said, 'Just do it; I think this guy has got the sophistication to manage.'" Today Mahindra & Mahindra is the fastest growing auto company in South Africa. "That would never have happened if we were rigid in those structures."

Similarly at Trip.com Group, Jane Sun likes to tell the story of a colleague who was hired at graduation from high school as a receptionist and subsequently promoted to be a supervisor, a manager, and a director.

The development of people has two core elements to it. One is role-modeling, coaching, and mentorship from the top. The other, which speaks to Mahindra's point about not putting people in boxes, is stretching staff through opportunity and challenge.

Role-Modeling: Leading by Example in Developing Staff

Asian founder-entrepreneurs pride themselves on leading by example. They see themselves as mentors and role models, helping to develop employees by showing through personal example what they wish them to be.

Aside from providing stretch opportunities like new initiatives and job rotation, which we will discuss next, there are perhaps three elements to leading by example. One is the role-modeling practice of being the visible embodiment of an attribute one wishes to see. So, for example, Midea's Fang Hongbo has a strong personal conviction that "bureaucracy and formalism are the greatest enemies of innovation," which is why he developed the management philosophy he calls *simplify for growth*. He role models this by promoting minimalism in management and practicing what he preaches, reducing the layers of management around him to four, and limiting executive meeting remarks to five minutes.

A second is support and problem-solving. This includes serving as a safety net for employees as they develop, providing psychological support and not shying away from getting into the details. A good example here is Bajaj Finance, which periodically surveys its front-end employees, asking them the top 10 problems making their lives difficult. Senior leaders personally review this feedback, correcting processes, removing bureaucracy, and at times even taking policy action.

A third is giving the sense of being in the trenches with employees, which is one reason Macquarie's Nicholas Moore made sure his office was glass-sided, facing a transparent internal lightwell and visible to as much of the bank as possible, when Macquarie was developing new premises to move into on Sydney's Martin Place in 2012. "All 2,000 people could see me at work," he says. "As a manager, I was always on display to the people I worked with."

This structure, he felt, conveyed Macquarie's key values of opportunity, accountability, and integrity. "Daylight's the greatest disinfectant, and if you're in an open plan environment where everyone's listening to what you're doing, the chance of you doing anything wrong without everyone knowing about it is very small."

Others practice this principle by being available, and sometimes working with the front lines in times of stress: Jane Sun joined her customer-facing sales teams at Trip.com Group during the COVID-19 pandemic, for example.

Mapping Talent from the Top

It's one thing to decide that talent should be molded within rather than hired externally. But how? What's the technique to shape people into what a founder wants them to be?

Akio Nitori has a useful perspective. Nitori says his company today is the number one for recruitment in all of Japan,[1] though it wasn't always like this. In the company's early years he just could not keep staff: they couldn't cope with the constant complaints from demanding high-end consumers in Japan unhappy with the products Nitori was sourcing from elsewhere in Asia. Only when the oil crises of the 1970s completely changed the availability of jobs – by which time Nitori was on its fourth intake of university graduates – did people start to stay.

Today, though, Nitori has mastered two skills: developing new talent, and delivering a message to graduates that the company is a place to grow. One thing we can learn from this is that true employee development must start at the top. Akio himself maps the skills that promising people have and tries to find a path for the best of them to reach the president level by the age of 50.

Even for those who don't reach so high, employees at Nitori can expect a sophisticated program of rotation, education, and observation. Development techniques are formalized through the Akio Nitori Management School, which teaches 1,200–2,000 people per year, 6–10% of the workforce.[2] But beyond this is something more distinct: Nitori has inculcated a willingness to confront in a society known for conformism. "From student to employee, I have them find problems, analyze, judge," he says. "Identify causes, propose countermeasures – immediate fixes or fundamental reforms. That's mandatory."

Stretching Talent

There are two distinct underlying schools of thought that apply to the development of talent. One is that every employee can succeed, given the right support and environment. The other is that there is a performance ceiling each individual has: bluntly, that some cut it and some don't.

Many founders tend more toward the first point of view, that everyone can excel given the right backing from the company. So they stretch their best people with ever-increasing responsibilities.

Some refer to this as strength-based leadership: the idea that every employee has a combination of distinct strengths that allow them to perform at their best, and that a workplace gets the best results when it magnifies these strengths.

Sidney Lu at Foxconn, for example, sets a high bar for people, but combines it with real support, believing that people develop when they are challenged and trusted with meaningful opportunities. "You've got to give them chances," he says. "Let them have their moment to shine. Challenge them, and in the meantime support them."

"The best environment for talent is a place where they feel comfortable, where they can truly show what they're capable of, and where they know there are people behind them to back them up," Lu says.

Daniel Tsai at Fubon expresses stretching as developing people from executors to problem-solvers. "When you try to solve a problem, you're forced to think deeply, and a lot of innovative ideas come out of that thinking process," he says.

"The problem with many people is that they're only used to executing tasks. They're afraid to do things they're not good at. But if you don't try things you're not good at, you'll never become good at anything." In a fast-evolving world, people must challenge themselves to be good at different things at different times, he says.

When this works, it leads to an inspired workforce delivering at the peak of their ability – perhaps beyond what they thought their ability was. "If we are to maintain talent, we have to give them something very challenging to do," says Suphachai Chearavanont, third-generation leader at CP Group. "With opportunity, if they succeed, it's almost like incubating a start-up."

Suphachai knows this from experience: he became a CEO in the telecoms arm of the business at the age of 30, in the middle of a restructuring following the Asian financial crisis. The debt-to-EBITDA ratio was 13 times when he took the top job. "I learned the hard way," he says.

And if founders and their descendants are given these demanding stretch challenges, the approach then perpetuates through the business. Young leaders are given ownership of new markets, ventures, and stores within the group to test their leadership early and under genuine pressure. "Rotate the people," he says. "Don't let them stay in the comfort zone and don't let them stop learning."

They are stretched through systematic rotation, just as employees are at Nitori, where they are assigned to unfamiliar functions and overseas operations to accelerate learning through discomfort. The same model is applied at Midea. Rotation is an example of a broader attempt to create specific opportunities for people, which might include special initiatives, new projects, or a whole new job.

Many of the founders in this book talk about the bold steps they have taken in developing employees and hoping they can cope. Uday Kotak, for example, says, "we took enormous amounts of risks on people" in the responsibility he gave to people in the early days as the bank was growing and finding its feet. "And fortunately, it worked for quite some time." People stretched, and proved themselves.

Once a supportive corporate environment is created, the benefits can be scaled across a workforce. The goal here is to "become a factory for talent of the kind you want both culturally and talent-wise," says Mahindra. "And therefore you need to create a system which is very strong in interventions and training, so there is a strong trajectory to fast-track people."

Doing so is particularly important because of the hiring pressures we addressed previously. As Joseph Tsai at Cathay Financial says, "It's hard to imagine you're going to be able to get 55,000 top talents" – Cathay Financial's headcount – so without correct development, the grow-your-own-timber model just won't work. "So create an environment where the work is meaningful. You're going to learn. You're going to grow."

Empowerment and Freedom

Founder-led companies are notable for giving people the empowerment to try, and sometimes to fail. Even if the reality is that these are top-down organizations with centralized decision-making led by the founder, it is important that people feel they have freedom to act with independence and to own their decisions.

This is why Tanimura at M3 speaks of creating an environment "that feels as close to being a business leader as possible" so that individuals feel both trusted and advanced. It's easier to set a stretch goal for someone who feels like they're being treated as a leader – and the reverse is also true. "When the bar is set low, the results tend to be mediocre."

Tanimura's views on individual accountability stand out in the hierarchical structures commonplace in Japan. He tells his people to accept accountability, and even when told to do something, to build a sense of ownership. "We believe that if you simply follow orders and fail, it's not the person who gave the orders who's responsible – it's you, because you're the one who knows the most about the situation," he says. "You need to think for yourself and take responsibility."

"If you see the world this way, there's nothing that isn't your responsibility. It makes work more enjoyable, because there are no excuses."

In Australia, Macquarie's view of talent management is closely aligned to its approach to risk management, encapsulated by the slogan: fail to succeed. We discussed the risk side in *Bold but Bounded*, but the other side is this: throughout its history, people have been encouraged to go out into the world and build businesses. They are given sufficient backing to make their ideas work – but not so much that they cause any lasting damage to the broader enterprise if they go wrong. Mistakes are encouraged, provided they are seen as an investment in learning and getting it right the next time. Macquarie believes the trust involved in giving individuals this freedom is part of what builds them as professionals, and is central to the whole company ethos. And its whole system of evaluation rests on this structure.

Fang Hongbo at Midea also speaks at length about ensuring staff are empowered to make decisions and, if necessary, fail. Midea has implemented a partner system to link core employees' interests with the company's success, aiding their transition from what Fang calls "professional executives" to "entrepreneurial partners." This is partly through performance-based stock ownership, where participants bear profits and losses just like any other shareholder, but it's also about a mindset of accountability in which employees understand they can get things wrong without censure so long as it's for the right reasons.

Trust and empowerment create the right environment for employees to try new things, to the good of the company, for they understand that if they fail, they will be assessed for the intention.

How to Challenge the Constraints of Boxes

We started this section with an objection to putting people in boxes – for how can they be stretched when there are walls in the way of extension? But avoiding a boxed mentality requires practical method. It's now common practice to attempt this, but founders have intuitively known this for some time.

In the mid-2010s, Bajaj Finserv created a common set of employee bands, or compensation ranges, for its operating companies, including creating a common talent scorecard for people in leadership roles. The talent scorecard maps the capabilities, aspirations, and progress on leadership and functional areas from one- to three-year perspectives. This enables greater career mobility not only within the company but also across the group.

Mobility is encouraged across levels: an online internal job placement program allows employees to apply for open roles across group companies. Existing managers can't block this: if someone is selected for a particular role, the boss in the current role has 90 days to make it happen. "So the bureaucracy, the idea that the boss can hold you back, doesn't apply," says Sanjiv Bajaj.

In implementing this system, Sanjiv made sure the holding company did not occupy some elevated position above other group companies. "I did not want the holding company to become this dominant parent directing underlying operating companies on what to do," he says. "I've seen too often with other large groups that the guys who make it to the holding company believe they are the cat's whiskers and know everything."

So people can move not only within operating companies but also to and from the holding company without friction.

This has been going on for long enough that Bajaj can now highlight some high-profile examples of it in action. The group chief financial officer (CFO) at Bajaj Finserv had previously been CFO of two different group companies, in life and general insurance.[3] Today he's proof of the capacity for advancement through internal rotation: of not being constrained by a box.

Sanjiv Bajaj says that this policy is extremely helpful in personnel development. "We like people to move around," he says. "We don't want them to be just vertical guys, because you become good leaders when you get that all-rounded experience."

Elsewhere Nitori rotates potential future president candidates through departments for one to two years at a time, gaining new skills and experience. And at Midea, mid- to senior-level managers must rotate across at least two departments to gain "hands-on, ground-level experience," according to Fang Hongbo. For successor candidates 90% must go through cross-functional training and development.

Taking this theory to its extreme, some founders are prepared to build new boxes for the right people, and to smash the old ones. David Ku argues so strongly that "this is a talent-led organization" that he is prepared to bend WeBank's whole model to accommodate them.

"If we see somebody really talented, we're even willing to change the organization for that specific person instead of forcing people to fit," he says. "Our business model is people driving it, it's not the strategy driving it."

Chapter Fifteen

I Take a Through-Cycle Approach to People

"If you are too unforgiving, nobody will try anything new because they want to avoid making mistakes."

—Wee Ee Cheong, UOB

At the opening of *Bold but Bounded*, we heard Dilip Shanghvi explain his current account and savings account formula. He was speaking of a holistic approach to people, evaluating them over the long term rather than only recent performance. That's what we mean by a through-cycle approach: an assessment that considers the highs and lows, both in terms of individual performance and the external environment within which people operate.

Shanghvi's approach, while distinctive in its imagery, is not uncommon among Asian founder-entrepreneurs, who tend to bring their long-term thinking to talent development as much as they do the overall business. At the leadership level, performance will be evaluated not through sharply defined scorecards so much as a considered overview of how people are developing and contributing, in a way that can tolerate missteps more than is common in Western companies. (Evaluation of front-line personnel can be more formulaic and quantitative: we are speaking chiefly of higher-ranking talent here.)

Wee Ee Cheong, third-generation leader of Singapore's UOB, thinks this attitude is particularly important for any institution that wants to retain an entrepreneurial mindset. With the exception of clear non-performers, "I don't believe in hiring and firing people," he says. "In the long term you have to forgive and forget" when people make mistakes in their entrepreneurial decisions. "Otherwise you want to have your cake and eat it. This way you build the muscle that is the younger generation."

When Wee talks about having your cake and eating it, he means that it's unfair to expect people to adopt the innovative risk profile of an entrepreneur if the structure of the company will penalize them for doing so. Anyone who thinks a single mistake will see them cast out of an enterprise – or at least impeded in their prospects – will never take the bold step that could lead to such a mistake. When that happens, the company misses out on the positive outcomes that would likely follow from ambitious efforts. So if mistakes happen in the attempt to achieve something good for the company, then the intent must be taken into account when deciding on what to do about the employee.

"If you are too unforgiving, nobody will try anything new because they want to avoid making mistakes," Wee says. "They will leave it to the boss to decide, and then you can't grow."

All of this speaks to a distinctive approach to evaluation, retention, and reward. And with senior talent evaluated in the aggregate – with success, failures, mistakes and triumphs considered collectively over the long term – we might consider it this way: it's about the movie, not the trailer.

Retention and Evaluation: The Asia Compact and Family as Foundation

In understanding why Asian founders tend to think this way, it is useful to understand a distinct difference in expectation for company behavior toward employees in Asia. The tendency of companies in Asia to upskill employees rather than make them redundant is part of a broader compact between employers and employees in Asia that is perhaps most potent among founder-led companies. They show loyalty, they back people, they offer stability, and they seek to be a lasting presence in the lives of their people. And in return they expect those people to stay.

Mukesh Ambani, for instance, inherited a distinct frame of mind from his father. "His philosophy was: I will make my employees my family, not make my family my employees," he says. "We always had the culture of saying that once you are part of us, we take care of everything."

If any of Reliance's 350,000[1] workforce has a wedding, it is expected that their boss, and probably their boss's boss, will be there. If anyone has a death in the family, the company not only offers support but expects to be the first to provide it. Reliance employees benefit from support services include an emergency response unit, comprehensive health insurance that includes parents and applies post-retirement, childcare support, and generous maternity leave cover – plus marriage loans and cash gifts, enormously important culturally in India.[2] "We will look after you," Ambani says. "This is not just lip service: it's what being part of the Reliance family means." (See "Involving Spouses: The Mahindra Universe Program" for another example of involving family in corporate responsibility.)

Reliance is an example of a common attitude among Asian founder-led companies: that loyalty is a two-way street. Anyone who expects loyalty from their employees must offer it equally to the workforce.

Involving Spouses: The Mahindra Universe Program

A truly holistic view of an employee includes their family. With this in mind, when Anand Mahindra developed the Mahindra Universe Program with Harvard Business School (it is now switching to Oxford University), he insisted that spouses be invited to the event.

Anand assumed that people's spouses would be asking them why they were joining an Indian company. "The thing we don't take into account is that when people go home, the first people who know about what's driving anyone in our company is their spouse. We pretend they don't exist, we don't talk to them, we don't ask their advice, we don't involve them." So he insisted that spouses be allowed to join.

There are good reasons beyond decency to behave this way. Retention matters more in Asia than elsewhere because of the labor force dynamics. Lose your people, and it's far from automatic that you will find equivalents to hire in the market, because there aren't enough candidates and they are tough to prise from their existing employers.

It also matters because one of the greatest challenges facing founder-led companies is to grow without losing their entrepreneurial spirit. It's partly for this reason that companies make such sustained efforts to embed and deepen culture so it doesn't get lost along the way. That can only work if people who understand that culture are retained for the long term – and evaluated holistically. When enough people leave, culture walks out the door with them.

Rewards and Incentives

Asian founder-led companies feel that part of the reward their employees gain is not financial: it is backing, loyalty, the ability to grow and stretch.

But the most obvious way to keep people at a company while they develop is money, no different from anywhere else. Our interviewees vary in this regard: some pay modestly and hope staff benefit in other areas, some supplement pay with option schemes, and some are unashamed about being the best payers in their field. "Compensation is still a very important tool to motivate people in privately owned companies," says Jeffrey Li, whose GL Capital is a private equity firm. "We are in a market economy, and people get compensated by how much they can contribute."

Macquarie pays so famously well that bonus day is closely watched in the Australia's media and the bank has attracted the moniker *the millionaires' factory*. "You get to share in the rewards of the business," Nicholas Moore says. "Macquarie pay, as long as I've been there, has been famous, front page of the newspaper. A lot of our people have made a lot of money and we think that's a good thing, particularly as it means our shareholders and clients have done well."

Macquarie is also one of many employers in this book who believe in tying their people into the business by making much of their remuneration not about cash but shares and options. Moore never sold a share while at Macquarie,[3] and his successor Shemara Wikramanayake has never done so either[4]; many Macquarie alumni are the same. This is why one of the biggest blocs on the shareholder register is current and former employees.

Plenty of others are similar. Jane Sun at Trip.com Group says she tries to create "an ownership culture," including incentive plans to employees who bring added value. "That structure works very well because then it's more long term." Doing so aligns employees' interests with those of the founders and shareholders. "Now everyone will say every penny we save is a penny we earn. I own a piece of the company." Infosys is another company known for its employee stock option plan.

In founder-led companies, incentives can assume a quite different hue to financial bonuses common in professional multinationals. They might include financial security for an employee's family or a one-off gift for performance – even a house is not unheard of.

Some businesses in Asia that have blended local and international expertise have a balancing act to perfect. At Techcombank, for example, the swift development of the Vietnamese banking opportunity, coupled with the lag waiting for skilled labor to catch up, made this combination a necessity – with a problem: expats had far higher salary expectations. "When local Techcombank staff members only earn maybe one fifth of an expat, an expat will think, 'Okay, you are a local, you are not very capable,'" Ho says. "The local will say, 'You don't really outperform me, why is your income five times higher than mine?'"

This problem was addressed, eventually, through natural improvement: as domestic capability stepped up, so did the associated pay. "That was a big challenge but the gap has narrowed," he says. "The income has started to converge and so has the knowledge." He takes great pride in the growth of personal wealth at Techcombank. "We have hundreds of millionaires, with very high income. And that's why they are becoming more loyal."

Reflective Questions

Derive Extraordinary Outcomes from Talent

1. What do you value when you hire externally and how are you increasing their odds of success?
2. How are you staffing your highest potential people against their greatest stretch opportunities to accelerate their development and maximize performance?
3. What is your personal model of unleashing the performance from your people? (For example, do you act as a quality check, role-model, mentor?)
4. What is your reward and recognition model that meets the test of being holistic and timeless?

Scale Without Losing Soul

"We try to be a startup at national scale"

—Mikhail Lomtadze, Kaspi

Governing Mindsets

- **I want to preserve my entrepreneurial core.**
- **I strive to manage business transition and family.**
- **I build an institution that outlives me.**

It is 1968 and in the small town of Shunde, south of Guangzhou between the channels of the Pearl River delta, He Xiangjian has an idea. He sees the coming shift from a rural China to an urban one powered by consumption, and he leads a team of 23 farmers to set up a factory. It is called Beijie Office Plastic Production Group and it will make plastic caps for bottles. Later, after entering the dawning home appliance industry in China with the manufacture of electric fans, the company will gain a new brand name: Midea.

Almost 60 years on from He's cooperative bottle cap idea, Midea is a Fortune 500 company with more than 190,000 staff and a business that covers more than 200 countries and regions, and 640 million global consumers.[1] It has gone from being a consumer goods specialist to a pioneering leader in smart living and the Internet of Things, supported by 38 global research and development (R&D) centers.

The journey between these two positions provides us with a remarkable example of scaling, and also illustrates a challenge that Midea had to overcome. How does one grow a business so dramatically without losing the entrepreneurial character that made it successful in the first place?

It is easy enough to chart the path Midea took. From those electric fans in 1980 it diversified horizontally and vertically in home appliances, moving into air conditioners, refrigerators, rice cookers, water heaters, microwave ovens, and dishwashers. It saw a gap in core components such as electric motors and compressors, and filled that market, too. It went thoroughly international, first through cautious overseas visits, then cooperation with Japanese and American brands, then mergers and acquisitions of some of those brands. It grew R&D capability and added it to existing competence in manufacturing, sales, and operations. And then it turned to technology, dominating the smart home service ecosystem space. Today it considers itself a global technology group more than a home appliance brand.[2]

So that's what Midea did. But how did it do so, culturally? Like many companies, Midea is filled with mantras, sayings, slogans, but perhaps the single most important is its management philosophy, "Simplify for growth." This stands for a commitment to eliminate bureaucracy that impedes decision-making, to exit the clutter of non-core businesses, to strip out activities that don't create value. This simplicity helps to preserve the culture that made Midea what it is. "I have always believed that bureaucracy and formalism are the greatest enemies of innovation," says Fang Hongbo, who joined Midea in 1992 and took over as CEO in 2012.

Midea, like so many other companies scaling up from small founder-led beginnings, understood the need to protect an entrepreneurial ethos as it grows. But what does this mean? What truly needs to be protected?

Chapter Sixteen

I Want to Preserve My Entrepreneurial Core

"It gets tougher as you get bigger."

—Sanjiv Bajaj, Bajaj Finserv

All leading Asian founders say some variation of the following: that it is important to try to preserve an entrepreneurial core while growing. That one of the greatest challenges is to scale a business without losing sight of the things that made it great in its earliest days: daring, agility, enthusiasm, belief. Among this group, the word *professionalism* carries negative connotations, as if it suggests a surrender of that initial swaggering fearlessness.

What is it that they're trying to protect? Anand Mahindra helps us to understand. "In my opinion, we never became purely professional," he says.

What does an entrepreneur want? Mahindra says the first thing is that they don't want to work for someone else all their life. "That's a very strong DNA in an entrepreneur," he says. One could call this a desire for power or independence, but Mahindra prefers the word *autonomy*. The second thing about entrepreneurs, he says, is that they are creative – not necessarily either left- or right-brained, but people who just have to create because it's in their nature. And the third is seeking wealth for themselves.

As he looks at Mahindra & Mahindra's history, Anand sees that his predecessors worked hard to preserve these attributes as the company grew. "Right from the start, Keshub gave everybody in leadership their autonomy," Anand says of his uncle, the second-generation Chairman of Mahindra Group. He recalls a former colleague, an Executive Assistant, who after leaving the group said how much he missed walking into the office every day with a feeling that he owned the company. He expressed gratitude for having been able to feel that way.

"So what had we given him? That autonomy. And once you give autonomy, you're also giving room for creativity."

One way Anand grants authority is to recognize that he doesn't have the right to tell anyone else what they should think or believe. "I don't think any one leader should have a monopoly over vision," he says. "If you're running your business, you have autonomy. And when it comes to vision, you have the autonomy to refine it or to define what your own vision is. I will not be looking for clones of myself to come in."

Anand tells us some important things about the characteristics that must not be lost through expansion. He speaks of autonomy, creativity, control. To these we can add the attacker mindset that comes from an underdog position: an us-against-the-world attitude that is fearless and disruptive, capable of achieving great things forged from the sense that others might not think them achievable. When underdogs get too big for that term to be appropriate – when they become the establishment and face a whole new generation of underdogs – then there is a challenge to keep that attacking, daring spirit alive.

Entrepreneurialism, as we have already learned, is about risk, determination, and hustle: of not being afraid to take a chance on a big idea even when starting out with little more than gumption and belief. All of these attributes are precious and should not lightly be lost with scale. They represent the soul of the entrepreneurial company – the soul of the founder.

So what are the potential pitfalls of scale?

The EE to PP Spiral

There is a vortex into which a growing company can fall. If we can define it, we can consider how founders avoid it.

Think of a four-stage life cycle in the growth of an entrepreneurial company: from fully entrepreneurial (EE) to entrepreneurial-professional (EP), to professional-entrepreneurial (PE), to fully professional (PP).

A new business starts out with vivid entrepreneurialism. These are the fun, daring, unfocused times, filled with unbridled possibility, albeit probably without a great deal of structure and planning. People, often young, running around in all directions, making things happen, not sleeping, lacking in process, and making mistakes but creating something new.

That phase is exciting and boisterous, but if an entrepreneurial company is not to burn out with its potential unrealized, then it must grow – and grow up. So in this second stage, it becomes what we might call an entrepreneurial-professional company. This is a good thing. During this phase, new people are inducted and the business begins to gain scale. As it does so, some professionalization is introduced and systems and processes develop. Performance reviews are formalized, perhaps with scorecards – a cadence forms for planning. It is still an entrepreneurial company and still has the zest it started out with, but with some infusion of professional skills, systems, and processes. That's why founders tend to talk about being like big startups; Mikhail Lomtadze, for example, says he runs Kaspi as "a startup at national scale," while Techcombank's Ho Hung Anh speaks of "a startup in a corporate."

"For us, there's no conflict between these two concepts [startup and corporate]," Ho says. "As a corporate, you need a foundation. You need professionalism. But if you are too much into processes and policies and frameworks, you miss out on creativity and innovation as well as engines for growth."

Things start to get more difficult as growth leads to the professional side dominating the entrepreneurial. This third stage brings an organization run by professionals who know how to run processes and systems. There are pockets where entrepreneurialism still finds room for expression, but fewer than before.

The danger to be avoided is what happens to some companies – not all – in the fourth stage, when they are entirely professional. It might not sound a bad thing to be professionally run, but many large companies find that as they have scaled successfully and become global, they have lost some of their entrepreneurial spirit. Bureaucracy is prevalent, energy depleted, and the previous bias to action subdued. Ossification can take place. There are certainly large companies that have worked to keep that entrepreneurial vigor alive but the danger of becoming big and dull must be guarded against.

The holy grail of scale is to keep your soul as you grow. It is extraordinarily difficult to shift from 10 people to tens of thousands without losing some of the energy, pace, and efficiency of those early days, but Asia's leading founder-entrepreneurs know they must try, because the essence of what they started with must always remain the heart of who they are.

The Right Kind of Growth

It's also worth remembering that growth is not automatically a good thing if it's the wrong kind of growth. Michael Kim at MBK says, "I would argue scale is more important than growth, and they're different." What does he mean? Growth, he argues, is a matter of mathematics: in his case, his assets under management going up. "I consider quality development more important than growth," he says. "People focus so much on GDP [gross domestic product] growth in every economy in Asia without thinking about the quality of that growth."

This is relevant because a very easy way to lose a company's soul is just to chase growth in any direction without thinking about what it means for competence, culture, or strategic direction. Kim is extremely selective. He has always found the idea of Asia as a homogenous region ridiculous, which is why MBK has focused exclusively on North Asia, chiefly South Korea, Japan, and Greater China. Expanding outside of that would mean "our competitive advantage erodes." In practical terms, this focus means MBK moves into businesses only where it has expertise, even if it's an adjacent expertise (like building a new special situations business, but only in North Asian geographies with which they are already familiar). So it can preserve its soul, but still scale – carefully. (See also "Challenging Cultural Norms at Trip.com Group" for another example of cultural norms affecting scale.)

Scaling also requires careful consideration of funding and timing, and this must be communicated to stakeholders to ensure that they are not surprised or disappointed along the way. CP Group's Suphachai Chearavanont notes the distinction between scaling in an evolutionary way from an established business and trying to do something new. "If you're doing something that adds value or evolves from your existing base, then you can talk about one, two, three years," he says. "But if you're starting something totally new, don't expect results in that time." He believes patience in a new venture is enhanced by raising the capital up front. "That gives you confidence. If not, you keep chipping in capital endlessly."

Challenging Cultural Norms at Trip.com Group

Scaling invites cultural challenges. In Asian societies, there is a greater respect for authority than is commonplace in the West today. This tends to reinforce hierarchical, often patriarchal models, both in society and in the workplace. This can impede the development of staff and stifle their willingness to innovate and to challenge. An entrepreneurial company might start out with go-getters who want to challenge the status quo, but how does it preserve that attitude as it scales in an environment where society tells them to do the reverse?

Trip.com Group is one company that has tried to get newer staff to think differently. "Internally we have lots of young people, so we encourage them to challenge," says Jane Sun, knowing this is against cultural norms. "In a typical Asian country, you respect the authority."

One unusual barometer of this success, she says, is when Chairman James Liang tries to leave the building. Frequently he can't get in the elevator, and he has no special right to do so ahead of anybody else. "The employees will say, 'Hey, James, you have your own car. We have a bus to catch. Can you let us in first?" Liang frequently finds himself walking down 10 floors instead.

There is a point to this. "It's important because in day-to-day life, if they see you as an equal person, during a debate they will raise their voice," Sun says. That represents not only development as employees but also an important contribution to decision-making. "These are the people on the front line. They know what's going on."

Preserving that attitude in young staff gives the company a decent chance of maintaining its aggressive, can-do attitude as it expands.

The Power of Successful Scaling in Asia

Research tells us that a company that scales with its soul intact tends to do extremely well. Companies experiencing hypergrowth – that is, 20–40% compounded annual growth – succeed when they align talent, structure, and culture with their scaling strategy.[1] A strong culture is a competitive advantage in scaling. Founders report that focusing on culture leads to better working methods and reduced attrition, which are essential for scaling.[2]

Preserving soul through growth is particularly important because of the extraordinary pace with which Asian businesses scale. Even though many don't operate across the continent, their home markets alone represent huge opportunities. Asia is the only place that has domestic markets of more than a billion consumers and has eight countries of over 100 million population,[3] huge home-grown bases to sell to. When combined with an ability to learn from best practice overseas, apply it to products manufactured at home, and then build assembly processes with world-leading efficiency and scale, the continent has a clear edge for scaling.[4] We see it in Taiwan's progress in semiconductors and Toyota's in engineering, for example.

How Founder-Led Companies Scale with Soul

Working out how to keep a company's soul intact with growth should not be taken lightly. Unicharm, for example, tries to unify culture internally through slogans (NOLA and DOLA – necessity of life with activities and dreams of life with activities) and a mantra ("love your possibilities"), with its ethos articulated in a guide called the *Unicharm way*, available as an app in nine languages. In this way it attempts to articulate the spirit of the company's founders and preserve the culture they developed even as the company expands.

Takahisa Takahara, whose father founded the company, says it took about 25 years to formulate these mission statements.

Another technique is to invest heavily in the next generation to make sure they believe in a company's culture from an early stage so that they carry these values forward through their career. An example is Bajaj Finserv's 30 under 30 group, a young leaders program to identify promising young people and push them forward in the company's cultural style.

Similarly, Techcombank has developed a number of programs aimed at ensuring employees deeply understand its cultural values of customer-centricity, work efficiency, collaboration, self-development, and innovation. To get this message across, Techcombank has an internal group of change agents called REDS who act as cultural ambassadors for the bank. There are 300 of these employees, sponsored by Ho as Chairman.[5] They are chosen for their ability to communicate the vision of management and to convince others to do the same.

Break to Grow: Keep Businesses Small and Nimble

Another company that faced the challenge of preserving its culture while growing at pace is the Bajaj group. "It does get tougher as you get bigger, and now we are over 100,000 employees," says Sanjiv Bajaj.

One interesting approach to this is a principle Bajaj calls *break to grow*. "When we think a business line is getting too big or complex, we will break it up," he says. In consumer finance, for example, where the business used to advance about 100,000 loans per month, it now advances 4.5 million, an unmanageable number for a single team. So Bajaj broke this down into segments: loans for white goods (e.g., home appliances) and brown goods (e.g., TVs), and digital products, and then when that got too big, loans to buy mobile handsets, handheld devices, and so on. Loans for mobile handsets quickly became the biggest component, so then they broke it down again, one business line for the top 100 cities, one for the next 500. Each business has its own dedicated head with a broad set of boundary conditions and full profit and loss (P&L) responsibility. Numerous subsets always exist under a bigger function in a matrix organization.

Infosys is another example of a company that routinely breaks things up to keep them feeling small. The moment a business becomes too big at Infosys, the company cuts it into smaller units with their own P&L targets to preserve that sense of a manageable, nimble, entrepreneurial business.[6] The same principle is at work when Infosys decides it has enough development centers in one city and, instead of building more critical mass in one place, chooses to set up in another city instead.[7]

Fighting Silos

Another way of avoiding this drift with size is to fight against the development of silos. Mukesh Ambani is a great believer in cross-functional leaders and people working together without silos. "There's no room for corporate politics," he says. "Our business goal is always 10 times bigger than any one person."

GS Caltex has developed techniques to guard against silos too. CEO Saehong Hur set up a business council to delegate more power to executive members, and then assigned cross-business strategic agenda items to each of them. "In the past we had a kind of silo mentality among different business units," he says. "Today they are in charge of strategic agenda items for the corporation, not just his or her unit. They are becoming team members."

Listen to the Front Line

Bajaj Group's pragmatism in breaking up business lines is matched in its desire to stay close to the front line. "Two years ago we felt there was a danger in getting bigger, that the organization could get more bureaucratic," Sanjiv says. After surveying frontline employees about the problems they faced, Bajaj streamlined and automated processes, revised policies that had been made far from the front line, then did another survey a year later to make sure the changes had worked.

This ethos – of listening to people who actually face customers – is common among enlightened founder-led companies, and ensures that size does not have to be accompanied by a drift away from knowing what the customer wants.

Bajaj makes sure his frontline principles are embedded by ensuring younger staff often lead projects – as those near to the start of their career tend to be closer to the market. It's the familiarity of this cohort with face-to-face customer interaction that makes them so relevant to decision-making, and this is why giving younger people accountable empowerment plays a positive role in keeping a business on track with its original values as it grows.

"Through a number of these programs we have seen bright youngsters identify significant challenges and find solutions," Sanjiv says. "Hardly any of these programs are a result of external inputs."

Today, frontline empowerment can be seen regularly at times of stress: a natural disaster affecting crops, for example. If the government grants farmers relief from loans at a time of such stress, some farmers don't understand and think they should get relief from private sector loans, too, which might not be the case. For a financial services group like Bajaj, that's a problem, and they have learned that empowered leadership on the front lines is the best way of dealing with it. "In this case we had leaders who will take ownership of different cities and towns, go and sit there themselves, and understand and solve issues on the ground," Bajaj says. "It's important for us to empower the front-end person to deal with the customer."

The natural corollary of empowering the front line is stepping back behind the scenes. Daniel Tsai at Fubon is an example of someone who learned to adapt his role as his enterprise scaled. At first, when running Fubon Group's bank, he was very hands on, coming up with ideas, leading discussions on new products and services, surveying branch locations. "But over time, I realized I couldn't continue doing that," he said. "My colleagues probably noticed a big shift in my management style. I'm no longer trying to be the innovator myself or the one who always comes up with the brilliant idea."

He has specific techniques for this adaptation, starting with the ability to listen before speaking. "I offer my ideas in meetings, but I'm not the first person to step out and say, 'This is how we should do it,'" he says. He recognized that as the organization grew, bringing in people from different backgrounds and talents, he had to change. "You can't give very specific instructions on what to do every day once the organization becomes large."

Chapter Seventeen

I Strive to Manage Business Transition and Family

"Management isn't something that can be easily inherited."
—Itaru Tanimura, M3

One of the biggest distinctions between founders and professional CEOs is the number of hats they wear. Professional CEOs are primarily focused on the business. Without question, they have to consider all their stakeholders – investors, regulator, customers, competition – and they are expected to make decisions for the long term, but still the company is the entirety of their responsibility.

Founders need to do all of that, but also think about their own family – as well as wearing hats as owners and philanthropists, too. The whole time a founder is running a business, they should also be thinking of the future and the day they must hand it over. So they must prepare their family members at the same time as they evolve their business.

The closer they come to retirement, the closer they will be to a pivotal decision: does my successor exist within my own family or must we transition to professional management? And if a founder would prefer the successor to be from within the family, how do they ensure that the right range of experience is gathered before the time comes for a handover?

Many founders, otherwise highly capable, get it wrong. Founder transitions are not black and white, and they are never easy, nor fast.

Later we will discuss the practical steps founders must make to prepare their businesses to be handed over, which gives them the confidence that what they have built will be protected. But there are also patterns to succession failure that can be rooted in emotion or bias. Since founders have built their legacy and wealth through the businesses they have created, succession involves handing over that legacy to someone else for the first time in their lives, so it is natural that founders find this process difficult. It is radically different to a professional CEO preparing a business for a successor.

Common failures include the following.

- **They choose in their own image.** Instead of hiring or promoting the person the company needs, they have a natural bias to find a replica of themselves. This can blind them to the skill sets other personalities and backgrounds might offer.
- **They fail to balance business and family considerations.** They may, for example, make a decision that maintains harmony in the family or creates a role for family members, but which is not in the best long-term interests of the business.
- **They leave it too late to go.** Nobody has more skin in the game than a founder, but it's a problem if they have so much skin in the game they can't leave. This links to an ill-advised sense of mortality – their

belief that they will always be around leaves them insufficient time to manage succession effectively.

- **They don't give their successor space.** This applies particularly when a founder has failed to work out what the next chapter of their life is; lacking purpose, they then remain too closely involved after formally stepping down, and so stop their successor from being able to operate effectively.

We can see in our range of interviewees several different ways family have progressed within companies.

Our founders cover a range of ages, but also a range of positions within a dynasty. Some, like Akio Nitori, Kiran Mazumdar-Shaw, David Ku, and Narayana Murthy, are first generation. They invented their business and made it what it is.

Others, like Mukesh Ambani, Daniel Tsai and Takahisa Takahara, are second generation: they saw a parent start an enterprise, and they grew up watching it take shape. They clearly understand what went in to making it what it is and they carry that understanding in their attitude to stewardship.

Many of our interviewees are third or fourth generation: Anand Mahindra, Joseph Tsai, Suphachai Chearavanont, Sanjiv Bajaj, Saehong Hur, and Wee Ee Cheong. Ayala is seventh generation. All of these people knew they were inheriting a role in a dynasty, which presents both its own opportunity – wealth, an established business – and the challenge of proving themselves when the business itself is already proven.

Regardless of the generation, these leaders embody the same six behaviors we have explored in this book. But the challenges they tackle in execution are different.

First-generation founders face the daunting task of starting from scratch, but the freedom to shape their business as they wish. With that freedom to build what they want, they are often disruptive innovators, such as Murthy pioneering the global delivery model at Infosys, Ku bringing new digital financial services to Mainland China, and Lu wanting Taiwan to have a world-class connectivity business in the semiconductor supply chain. They often built their businesses through informal talent structures, bringing a core team together and trusting them to deal with new opportunities in the early days before creating more systematic policies.

As we turn to second and later generations, they have the benefit of systems and resources but the burden of evolution, with a bar forever rising from where it started. They are loyal custodians of the mission they inherited, but as they take it forward our interviewees have all found their own way to make a mark.

We see this in the endless reinvention of Reliance Industries under Mukesh Ambani and the steady acquisitive expansion of the Fubon Group under Daniel Tsai. But we also see the challenge of achieving this growth without losing the business's core identity, expressed through Takahisa Takahara's devotion to understanding the customer no matter how big Unicharm gets, taking every opportunity to meet them in person and learn from them.

Joseph Tsai saw what he could bring to Cathay Financial that had been unavailable to his predecessors. "My value add to the family business has probably been more around innovation and digitization," he says. And he's brought Western-influenced styles of management in to the mix, sometimes to his father's chagrin; he wants staff to engage in conversations, not just read PowerPoints to him.

But it's not easy for these people. Tsai is proud of the reputation his grandfather and father built, and keen to protect it. But he says that reputation is "a burden of the benefit" of inheriting an institution. The benefit is the scale and quality, but "it's a burden because that scale makes it a challenge to say, can I double this next year, or in 10 years?"

The Unexpected Family Business

Falguni Nayar runs Nykaa with her twin children, daughter Adwaita, CEO of Nykaa Fashion, and son Anchit, who is head of beauty and e-commerce. But this was not originally the idea.

"When I started, it was not really meant to be a family business," Falguni says. She happened to launch it at a time when her children were graduating, and the timing worked: one joined the business almost immediately and another five years later. Today, it feels very much like a family enterprise. "So all that motivation that I have for the mission, the vision, the excitement that I have toward the business, they share with me. It has become like a shared vision."

Just as the Tsai brothers at Fubon find great benefit from being around like-minded family, Falguni feels strengthened by her children. "The way I feel is that now I have three times the time and energy and ability to do it, with slightly different skill sets." It can be stressful, she says, but works because of the closeness of the family and a mutual respect for what each brings. "They are not getting equal credit as cofounders, but if you look at it today, they have a cofounder role, because I consult them for everything. Our structure is not one where I take the decision and everyone follows."

The family dynamic helps to cement a sense of responsibility to build a business robust enough to be passed through generations. "We are the long-term beneficiaries, but we are also going to be long-term guardians and custodians of this business."

Is the Next Generation Ready and Willing?

When it comes to handing over the top job, this obviously depends on circumstances. Some families are very structured. The Zóbel de Ayala family – who have both a family council and a family constitution to bring governance to their succession[1] – seem to be extraordinarily adept at it. The CP Group applies a structured family governance system through which the next generation is prepared for leadership by being placed into new markets to build experience. While family leadership is important at CP Group, the stated goal is to have the most capable person in charge, even if one day that is an outsider.

Others must deal with the fact that they know the next generation does not have the capability or desire to operate the business day-to-day. Often people like this become active owners, sitting on boards and appointing CEOs but not conducting day-to-day management. Others have a next generation that wants to do something totally different, and at this point someone outside the family must be appointed.

An example of a company where the next generation of a family will likely not take the reins is UOB, where Wee Ee Cheong does not expect to pass leadership to his children. "My children are not interested in managing the bank at this point in time," he says, adding that he would not force them to do so. "They love to do something else. They have their own careers and interests." While the next generation may not run the bank, Wee thinks that at some point they could serve on the board and help to continue some of the family's long-standing business philosophy.

This also appears to be the case at Techcombank in Vietnam. "I don't think the next generation, my children, can do the same thing I did," says Ho Hung Anh. "If I continue to maintain that culture, maybe my children are no longer excited, or not able to manage that. And then when the founder leaves, the organization cannot continue to grow. That's why for an organization to grow sustainably, professionalism is needed."

Some may pursue an interim step before returning to family leadership: at Sun Pharma, Dilip Shanghvi's son Aalok and daughter Vidhi are rising through the business (Chief Operating Officer and Executive Director, respectively[2]), but while they gather experience Shanghvi himself transitioned from CEO to Executive Chairman in September 2025 and appointed a trusted professional Kirti Ganorkar as Managing Director leading operations.

Challenges are amplified in what is known as a cousin syndicate, or at least multiple siblings. There are techniques to dealing with this, such as giving different siblings different swimming lanes with their own distinct responsibilities or rotating them over time. At Reliance Industries, for example, Mukesh Ambani carries on the vision of his founder father, but has also put great effort into readying his three children for succession. All three have clearly defined roles: Isha is in retail, Akash leads Reliance Jio Infocomm, and Anant Reliance New Energy. Each have separate boards running separate ecosystems.

An important point, often overlooked, is that treatment of the next generation – in terms of readiness, rotating portfolios, giving them specific businesses to run – should not just be for the departing generation to decide. It should be for the generation coming in to think about what they want to do and develop that in partnership with the founder. Second- or later-generation leaders already feel the great pressure of proving to the parent that they can live up to their expectations; in Asia, culturally, those parental expectations tend to be particularly high. They are further disadvantaged by the fact that if a company has been successful, then stakeholders will be hoping for something of a clone of the founder; that's not fair or realistic.

Fundamentally, the next generation must decide what sort of owner they want to be. Do they want to be owner-operators? Owners who have a more limited involvement? Do they want to sell their stake and do something else? Do they want to keep the stake but have no involvement, like a passive investor? It is better to be clear on these things from the outset than to realize 25 years later that there is more resentment between two generations than there is alignment.

Accepting that the Next Generation have their Own Minds

A further challenge for founders is that they can't tell anyone what to think or do after they've gone. What a founder wants to instill in the next generation is not necessarily what that next generation believes. Partly, this is pride: a second- or third-generation person will not want people to think they just acquired immense riches without any effort. They will want to put their own imprint on things and chart their own course.

Tanimura at M3 notes, "Management isn't something that can be easily inherited. It's not like kabuki," a traditional Japanese performing art where specific movements can be learned and replicated. "Even within the same family, times change, and even with shared DNA, strengths differ."

Anand Mahindra, as a third-generation member of a founding family, rebelled in early years, turning socialist and almost joining the Communist party, then studying film, partly to be different. "I went into something where Daddy couldn't help me," he says. "I made a film, hand-holding a camera, managed the soundtrack, everything myself." Clearly, this was rallying against expectation and assumption. "'You were born with a silver spoon, you're going to inherit what you do.' So I just had a very strong sense of ego: I didn't want to end up where somebody could tell me that I didn't do anything, it was all given to me." But what's interesting about this case is that Anand seems to have been given the agency to be a rebel for a while to figure himself out. If so, that was a good call, because the alternative is an unhappy, passive-aggressive next generation.

What Worked Before May Not Work in Future

We find several Asian economies at an interesting inflexion point concerning succession. In India, for example, the economy truly opened up only in the 1990s, so the people who founded companies then have spent more than 30 years at the top, are getting older, and are considering whether the next generation is ready to step up. Since Deng Xiaoping's "socialism with Chinese characteristics" reforms didn't really gather pace until the late 1980s, China is at a similar point to India in terms of the aging of founder-entrepreneurs. One sees the same patterns in South Korea, following market restructuring in the 1980s, and many Southeast Asian nations, where founders who cut their teeth in the 1997 Asian financial crisis are now almost three decades past that crucible moment.

China, India, and most Asian jurisdictions are completely different countries than they were in the 1980s and 1990s, to an almost unrecognizable degree. And what worked for founders then may not work now. Many – including several in this book – have charted this path very successfully by adapting, but there is often an argument that new blood may be better equipped to implement new ideas.

Some are receptive to this, but some have such strength of character and conviction that they can't believe others can be as successful as them because of what they have built. When a founder's personality is so clearly imprinted on a company, it's not just a business that is handed over but an idea. They built their identity on the company, they created it from nothing: how can they give it away? A founder with two children actually has three, with the business being the third offspring.

The Founder Bottleneck

This can be a problem: founders can become the biggest bottleneck to the growth of their organization by a refusal to move on. That, in turn, can lead to a next generation, which can be frustrated, sometimes to the point of stepping away from the company.

At this stage, founders are required to come up with a whole new skill set, as if the skills they required to build their enterprises weren't enough: the skill to disrupt themselves completely and step aside. It requires them to consider whether their continuing presence will limit the organization.

"A CEO who overstays is as bad for an institution as a CEO who doesn't stay long enough to transform an institution," says Uday Kotak.

There is a spectrum of readiness to do this among founders. On one side are those who are not aware of the risk of damaging a company by overstaying, and are not thinking much about succession as a consequence. The middle is aware but not sure what to do about it, and on the other side are those who are aware and are taking action. McKinsey's experience shows that a plot of this spectrum of readiness would have a big cloud in the middle. They know there is a need to change but have discovered it isn't easy to do so. And getting it wrong can have severe financial consequences (see "An Inevitable, Though Not Permanent, Value Destruction").

An Inevitable, Though Not Permanent, Value Destruction

McKinsey research shows that most transitions lose more value than they create for the first two years. In a study of more than 200 family-owned businesses, there was an average decrease of 5.7 percentage points in total shareholder return over a five-year period post-transition, compared to the five years pre-transition. Revenue and EBITDA margin growth go the same way. Only 35% of CEO transitions manage to increase TSR; 65% deplete value.[3]

This applies in family and nonfamily businesses, but is perhaps exacerbated in family businesses. The outcomes appear to be polarized: only 29% of transitions to family CEOs create value, compared to 39% to nonfamily CEOs. But transitions to family, when successful, have the potential to deliver outsized returns: the ones that do work generate an average of 23 percentage points in TSR increase, compared to 14 percentage points for value-creating transitions to nonfamily executives.

Organizing for Transition

Some are more equipped for this than they might think: they have recognized along the way of building their business that there are things they do very well, and things that they don't, and have sought expertise – from employees, partners, family members – to fill the gaps. Stepping aside is a difficult extension of that recognition.

When there is a systematic approach to keeping the same set of values alive throughout a company over time, succession issues are easier to manage.

"Rather than relying on individuals, we create systems," says M3 Founder Itaru Tanimura. "If you have 100 people with a sense of business acumen, that's enough for succession planning."

As part of building systems, the most successful transitions have been very deliberate about making sure the entire organization is ready for a transition.

Our final reflection is the work of preparing for transition can take anything from 5 to 15 years if done properly, in giving the right range of experiences to the next generation. But the point is that it's not about when a family starts discussing transition so much as when it starts acting on transition. It is not uncommon to find families who have been talking about transition for 20 years but have not actually done anything tangible about it. It takes time: it means preparing for change with the company, the family, the board, and for listed companies the market, too.

So what do family-owned businesses that have undergone successful transitions do differently? McKinsey research[4] tells us that five practices are particularly critical:

1. Consider and evaluate multiple candidates when selecting potential successors, from within the family, within the executive team, and externally.
2. Expose the successor candidates to well-rounded experience and capability across different areas.
3. Manage the transition like a project, involve multiple stakeholders, and ensure regular review of success against set goals.
4. Set up and adhere to a robust and aligned "transition out" plan for the incumbent.
5. Put in place credible and neutral governance mechanisms for both family and business; review them regularly and adhere to them even if difficult.

Chapter Eighteen

I Build an Institution That Outlives Me

"If what you build does not outlast you, you have failed."
—Uday Kotak, Kotak Mahindra

While founders can sometimes act as if they're immortal, they're not totally blind to the fact that their time will one day come to an end. And when it does, they tend to care deeply about how they will be remembered. Legacy matters.

Many of our interviewees talk about legacy with considerable pride, and were thinking about how they might be remembered from the moment they launched their businesses.

Consider Kotak Mahindra, which carries the names of two of our interviewees in this book. Uday Kotak said to Anand Mahindra in 1986: "Let's put our name on the line. It's our reputation." It was clearly motivated by a desire to create perpetuity, even though that came with a risk: one can just as easily attach one's family name to a failure as a success. Perhaps doing so is a way of putting skin in the game, not only financial but reputational, even emotional.

Kotak likes the idea of legacy expressed through a name. "Think about a JP Morgan, a Goldman Sachs, a Morgan Stanley: these are all family names," he says. "The families are long gone but the institutions have survived."

"There is a deep philosophy that we are building something great for ourselves, for India and for the world, and we must build things to last," he says. "Because if what you build does not outlast you, you have failed."

Perhaps it's a national characteristic because many Indian founders have a similarly passionate sense of legacy. Mukesh Ambani was given this guidance by his father. "At the end of the day you come into this world with nothing, and you leave with nothing," he says. "What you leave behind is an institution." His father told him that institution, Reliance, must outlast them both. "That's the commitment I have."

Having an ambition beyond one's own lifespan is, of course, not exclusively an Indian conceit, and is common among founders across the region. Saehong Hur says that at GS Caltex "I started with a vision: let's become a centennial company." In 2026, GS Caltex is 59, so this is an ambition that will outlive him, and that's how he believes it should be. "To reach 100 years, what do we need?"

"In Asia we believe there's a strong value in helping companies keep going for the long term," he says. "I'm not just looking at my generation. I'm looking at the next generation and the one after that. I want to create a company that can survive and sustain itself – not just for 100 years, but beyond. To achieve that, I need the right system, the right process, the right people, and the right culture in this organization."

Leaving the Legacy of an Institution

Anyone can pass a company on to somebody else. But are they passing on an institution, something that can not only function but also thrive for multiple generations?

McKinsey research has studied corporate longevity worldwide, and has reached conclusions on the practices that are at the heart of lasting institutional health.[1]

Businesses that build and preserve dynasties have some common ground, our research finds. They implement governance frameworks that protect from takeover, individual greed, or recklessness, with proper checks and balances in place.

Businesses with corporate longevity have specific initiatives to ensure a stringent process to identify future generations of owners, and to groom them to be world-class shareholders through training and business experience.

And they cherish and protect their freedom of decision-making by putting in place controls to ensure financial independence.

We can see good examples of these ideas in the approaches of our interviewees. On **governance**, for example, few things are more important when handing over an institution than the rules and practices that govern its everyday operations. The best founders make sure the right checks and balances are in place, that the board is in good shape with appropriate oversight, that financial reporting is transparent, and that risk management is robust.

CP Group is a good example, with a corporate governance committee combining members of the leadership and external experts and 12 governing principles. These principles include integrity, honesty, the role of boards, and – based on the principles – clear processes for training, corporate risk management, and whistleblowing.

On the point about identifying **future generations** of owners, many founders have sought to build a self-perpetuating leadership engine. That doesn't just mean identifying a successor but also having institutional mechanisms for later generations of succession planning and leadership development. For example, Bajaj maps the talent scorecards of people across all of its subsidiaries to keep track of their capabilities and their aspiration over multiple time frames. Then it provides technical or leadership training programs suitable to their level of promise.

Founders add two more elements to the institutional mix: **value to society** and an **entrenched culture**. It matters to founders that the business they pass on has, in its bones, the idea of being a force for good in the system within which it operates. An example of this principle at work can be found in Mahindra & Mahindra's mission statement, "together we rise." Fully articulated it says: "Drive positive change in the lives of our communities. Only when we enable others to rise will we rise." There should be a sense of purpose that has been absorbed by the company so completely that the mission won't drift when the leadership changes.

And founders want to make sure that the culture they have instilled is so clearly articulated that people at every level of their company understand the values they are representing. They know that strong culture is extremely resilient to the difficulties of transitioning a business from one leader to another.

GS Caltex, for example, has put great effort into creating a culture of alignment among the workforce even as they undergo transformational change to be more adaptable to shifting market environments. "We created a new model for our deep transformation journey, and it's not just short-term profit," says Saehong Hur. "It is more fundamentally that we want to change our culture and make people aligned with the same strategic direction." The level of thought that has gone into cultural considerations through this process will protect the company in the future.

Founders know this isn't easy. "Trying to think of myself as a professional manager, to help the company transform from a family-run business to a professionally run business, was the biggest hurdle for me," says Daniel Tsai of Fubon. "Being handed the responsibility to take the family business to the next level. That was the challenge."

Tsai does not think of himself as being a second-generation figure. Although he and his brother Richard inherited a family business established by their father Tsai Wan-Tsai – and "wanted to make him proud" – Daniel believes they did something radically different with it. "I like to think of myself not as a second-generation entrepreneur, but first-and-a-half," Daniel says. "We didn't just inherit business from our father. We created new businesses." The brothers transformed Fubon from primarily a property and casualty insurer into a multi-business conglomerate with significant international holdings over the course of more than four decades.

It is telling that when Daniel found his way in the business well before running it, he understood that family status was not enough, and that he wanted and needed the trust of professionals if he was ever to lead them professionally. "If I don't earn the respect from my management team – from all these professionals – I cannot lead," he recalls thinking. Well before taking on leadership of the company, he understood this imperative to transform a family business to a professional one.

All these are mechanisms not just to keep a dynasty intact but to pass a functioning institution forward.

Remembering History in Institutional Legacy

An important part of legacy is not just that a business continues but that its values are intact when the founder is gone. Founders consider their culture and history precious. That's natural: companies are an extension of the founders themselves, their dreams and their personalities, and their work ethic.

We started *Scale Without Losing Soul* with Midea's bottle-top factory. It's an appealing story for a big corporate to look back on: it speaks of entrepreneurial dreaming but also smart vision and hard work, and is a reminder that small beginnings can lead to mighty things.

Midea recognizes the asset that its history represents, and has put a lot of effort into keeping the company's values intact. Storytelling is a large part of the technique: making sure people know the history right back to He Xiangjian's bottle-cap workshop so employees understand the company's development journey.

"Midea has countless stories to tell," Fang Hongbo says. "The company's history, mission, vision, and core values together form the essence of the Midea story." It is told in different ways from group level to regional units, he says, "but the common goal is to help employees understand Midea and build an initial recognition of its development journey."

This will all matter very much as a matter of legacy as leaders succeed one another. No matter who is at the top, it will be easier to preserve a culture if it has been communicated throughout by storytelling.

Reflective Questions

Scale Without Losing Soul

1. How are you preserving the entrepreneurial core as you scale up?
2. How are you reflecting holistically on your succession (family members, internal candidates, external hires) to ensure a successful and sustainable transition?
3. How are you thinking about your legacy?

Epilogue

We have learned a great deal about the most successful founder-entrepreneurs, what makes them tick, and how we might apply these characteristics to our own work practices. They are remarkable people, but it is important to acknowledge that they are still human. As readers seek to learn from them, they should not try to imitate them wholesale: everyone is different, and there is no fixed recipe that will work for all people.

For some readers, the idea of hiring for character over competence will strike a chord and become a practice they can apply. Some will use what they have learned about a bifurcated approach to risk. Some of these attributes will be innate to individual founders, a product of the influences of their background, and therefore difficult for anyone else to truly replicate. And that is fine: it is enough to take an interest in their stories and admire their work.

Figure E.1 Shapers and founders: 6 behaviors and 18 mindsets

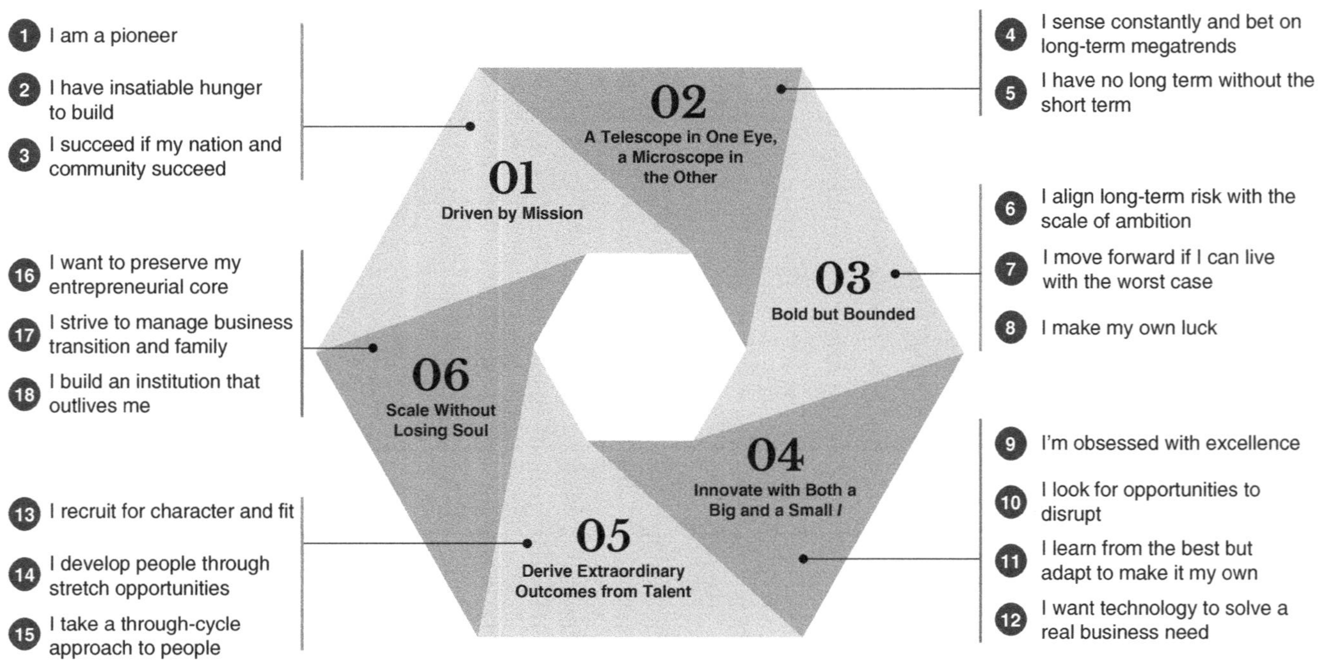

Implications

We hope this book will appeal to a wide range of audiences, and that each will take something different from it. Following are some takeaways and reflections for different groups.

Professional CEOs

We have learned that founder-CEOs are able to plan for a far longer time frame than professional CEOs since they generally intend to be in their business for life – and ideally the lives of their descendants, too. Through this, founders are able to take on a more missionary outlook in the development of their business. They are also, for better or worse, able to cut through unwieldy bureaucracy to effect faster decision-making. Ownership makes them less beholden to a board, for example, and also underwrites their continuity as a leader.

While the professional CEO cannot count on that degree of longevity in their business, nor the freedom to make quick, bold decisions, they can still apply some of these learnings. Indeed, many successful professional CEOs practice the techniques we have discussed in this book.

Former DBS CEO Piyush Gupta, and former Sony CEO Kazuo "Kaz" Hirai, are instructive examples. Gupta reframed DBS's purpose around "making banking joyful," embodying *Driven by Mission*. He also illustrated *A Telescope in One Eye, a Microscope in the Other* by betting early on digital transformation while consistently delivering near-term financial performance. Hirai is a transformational figure who took Sony from the brink of bankruptcy to a reputation for big-*I* innovation (his last bold move as CEO was to present the relaunched Sony Aibo robot dog in 2018, which broke new ground in AI, advanced robotics, and cloud connectivity). Both also embody *Bold but Bounded:* Gupta placing transformative technology bets before the rest of the industry followed him; Hirai backing new ideas like healthcare robots.

Neither founded their institution, yet both prove these mindsets can be chosen, not just inherited. Professional CEOs may therefore reflect whether they can apply long-term thinking to their own approach to leadership, even if they may not be the one to see it through. They might ask whether the cycle of quarterly or half-year reporting, and investor demands, have pushed them toward a more short-term way of thinking than is beneficial. Is their approach to hiring and talent helping to stretch and retain the best people, and if not, what can they learn from the founders? Are there areas where they may be too complacent about risk management and could place themselves in a discomfort zone to learn?

Finally, if the professional CEO works for successful founders, understanding the mindset and behaviors of those founders is critical to adapting their own style and approach to management. That will enable them to work with the founder in a partnership mindset, respectful of their history and leveraging their unique talents while bringing the professional's own true leadership to bear. And even if they don't work for them, they will need to compete with them in the marketplace.

Existing Founders

Existing founders will inevitably be comparing themselves to these giants of business and wondering how they measure up. It is not the intention of this book to elevate these founders so far that their success seems unattainable; rather, the hope is to illuminate their techniques so others might learn from them.

Existing founders might ask if they are still clear on the mission they started out on, and whether they have stayed true to it. They may reflect on how they balance short-term goals and their long-term road map, and whether they are still innovating with both the big and small *i* of innovation. They would benefit from examining their succession planning systems so that the business can be passed on, whether it's to their children or professionals. And they might ask if the company's soul has been diluted as they have grown – and what they can do about it if it has.

Aspiring Founders

We hope that new generation founders will be inspired by what they have read. The people in this book clearly represent good role models for any aspirant founder.

Aspirants reflecting on the book might ask themselves what their sense of mission will be: what matters to them beyond growth profitability. They might think about how stakeholder capitalism will be applied in their work, and how they will develop their attitude to risk. It is helpful to think from the outset about helping people realize their true potential, how the founder will avoid becoming a bottleneck that blocks the advancement of others, and how they will scale their business without losing the start-up culture and idealism with which they started. And they could consider their personal readiness for the journey ahead, recognizing that it might be bruising and all-consuming.

Beyond The Business Community

For the general public, business students, or those conducting management research, we hope that insights have been gained on a very distinct way of leading a business. In addition, they might ask what they can apply in their own life from what they have learned of the DNA of founders – dealing with ambiguity, investing time in continuous learning, building a web of strong relationships. They could ask how Asian cultural distinctions, including philosophy and history, have influenced the way these businesses are run, and what lessons might arise from that elsewhere in the world. It's also interesting to ask whether the same principles of talent management will work with Generation Z, and how their expectations of life and work will be reflected in the way businesses are run.

Founders have shown great resilience and adaptability, so we should expect their mindsets to evolve as change happens around them. It will be fascinating to watch that evolution take place, as a new generation of founders position for a shifting world.

Final Reflections

As Asia cements its restored place as the world's economic engine, the founder-led company will continue to be a vital fuel. Many of the ideas we have discussed in this book – a very long-term mindset guided by a sense of mission, a commitment to innovation in all of its forms, a nuanced understanding of risk that enables a company to bet big without risking its future – will become steadily more important across a continent that no longer needs to follow other markets or technologies, but can now lead. Asia will need the visionary thinkers, the market architects, those who know not only how to invent but also to scale and refine. As we enter into the next era of AI, this group of leaders will be ever more important, and their behaviors and mindsets worth reflecting over.

When the people in these pages are gone, they will leave behind a legacy on which Asian business and trade will continue to build. Decades from now, everyone from individual consumers to whole regional economies will still be benefiting from the spirit of daring and adventure they brought to a singular opportunity: to make something new that mattered.

Acknowledgments

This book belongs, first and foremost, to 30 owner-CEOs (see "The Contributors" section for more on them) who welcomed us into their offices, their boardrooms, and, in many cases, their homes. They shared not only their achievements but also their doubts, setbacks, and hard-won lessons with a candor that humbled us. Bringing their stories to the page, however, required the talent and commitment of many others.

Within McKinsey & Company, we were fortunate to have sponsors and thought partners who championed this work from the start. Shelly Stewart, Vikram Malhotra, Kurt Strovink, Alex Panas, and Becca Coggins provided the institutional backing and intellectual encouragement that kept the project on track.

An enormous thank you to Jennifer Chiang, who for all practical purposes is the fourth author of this book. Jennifer corralled the team behind the scenes, interviewed alongside us, spent countless hours bringing these stories alive, and sparred with us every step of the way.

None of this would have come together without the team who worked alongside us for the past year through every phase of this effort. An equally big thanks to Sharyn Lee, Cynthia Luan, and Harsh Nagar, who conducted research, distilling hundreds of pages of interview transcripts, and assembling the data points and case studies that give this book its foundation.

Their energy, precision, and good humor sustained the effort through many long stretches. We would also like to thank Sanchit Jain and Daisy Homolka from our research team, and Janice Tan, Yvonne Chan, Nurul Nawi, and Rori Ammen, who always ensured our logistics ran smoothly.

From the outset, we recognized that doing justice to the richness of these leaders' experiences would require more than analytical depth – it would demand compelling narrative and consistent voice. Chris Wright and the team at Resonate Global Advisors rose to that challenge. Chris was instrumental in shaping the book's architecture and voice, transforming dense insights into prose that we hope reads as vividly as the conversations that inspired it. His partnership elevated this project in ways we could not have achieved alone.

There are many more McKinsey colleagues we would like to give a special shout out to, including Jeongmin Seong from McKinsey's Global Institute, who contributed expertise on Asia's macroeconomic and historical context, and helped spar with us on our fundamental methodology to elevate our level of analysis. Our colleagues Joe Ngai and Nick Leung also lent their expertise on China from many decades of experience. Our colleagues in the People & Organizational Performance practice, including Acha Leke, Chaitali Mukherjee, and Gourav Ghosh contributed deep expertise on themes central to our book – family business governance, leadership succession, and the organizational complexities unique to owner-led enterprises. We also thank our many McKinsey colleagues – Alok Kshirsagar, Albert Chang, Frank Chu, Albert Lee, Mukund Sridhar, Noppamas Sivakriskul, Guillaume de Gantes, Vladimir Kulagin, Violet Chung, Kevin Wei Wang, Bruce Xia, Motohiro Hojo, Wonsik Yoo, Jae Jung, Aizhana Dostiyarova, Masanobu Kurihara, Jeehyun Shin, and Lei Xu – without whom many of these exclusive interviews would not be possible. And finally we thank our colleagues from McKinsey Center for CEO Excellence (MCCE) – Janice Koh, Siya Sood, Nakul Sharma, Aleia Chavez,

Trang Pham, and Chaitanya Parab – who have been a core part of the CEO excellence journey.

Raju Narisetti and Global Publishing guided us through the mechanics of turning a manuscript into a globally published book, a process that was new to all three of us. We are equally grateful to the editorial team at Wiley, Richard Narramore, Susan Cerra, Susan Geraghty, and others at Wiley whose professionalism and partnership made the final stages of production a genuine pleasure. Kathryn Hanes and the R&E team (Adrienne Cernigoi, Debbi Cheong, Cherise Lei, Jenna Bae, Jiny Chang, Georgia Peard, Josh De Guzman and Jeyachandran K), brought the fullness of their energy into turning an idea into something executable from the early beginnings to the final launch. Max Gleischman, John Pratt, and Sean Lloyd ensured that our work met the highest standards of diligence and reputational integrity.

Above all, we owe a debt to our families. This book was written in the margins – on flights, over weekends – while each of us continued to serve clients full-time. Our families absorbed the cost of that commitment with extraordinary grace, and we are deeply grateful for their patience and unwavering support.

Finally, to you, our readers: thank you for picking up this book. The stories within it have profoundly shaped our own understanding of leadership, and we hope they do the same for you.

The Contributors

Mukesh Ambani

About Reliance

India's largest public company by market capitalization (more than US$210 billion) and revenue (more than US$115 billion) as of December 2025. Today it ranks 88th on the Fortune Global 500 (2025)—the highest-ranked Indian company on the list

Leading conglomerate with interests spanning petroleum refining, petrochemicals, textiles, natural resources, retail, telecommunications, digital services, and green energy

Career Highlights and Impact

Chairman and Managing Director of Reliance since 2002; joined company in 1981. Under his leadership, the group has grown from a petrochemicals and refining business into one of India's largest consumer and technology platforms

Built and operates the world's largest single-site refining complex with 1.4 million barrels per day crude processing capacity with the world's highest Nelson complexity index of 21.1

Drove Reliance's strategic expansion beyond its petrochemical roots, establishing the nation's premier retail footprint through Reliance Retail with more than 20,000 stores, and committing over US$10 billion to a New Energy venture aimed at building a fully integrated clean energy ecosystem

Through Reliance Jio, which he launched in 2016, he has made affordable mobile data and digital services widely accessible across India; the network is now the country's largest mobile operator, with more than 500 million subscribers

Asia's richest individual (Forbes, 2026); first Indian to be named a rupee trillionaire in 2007

Aspiration to build India's sovereign artificial intelligence (AI) infrastructure through Reliance Intelligence, backed by a ~US$110 billion multi-year investment to enable affordable AI at national scale

Ho Hung Anh

About Techcombank

Founded in September 1993 and is headquartered in Hanoi, Vietnam

Highest average return on assets (ROA) of any Vietnamese bank between 2020 and 2024

Career Highlights and Impact

Chairman of Techcombank since 2008; led post financial crisis (2008) restructuring and transformation into a high-return retail and corporate banking business

Pioneered the zero-fee strategy in Vietnam's banking sector, spurring industry-wide change

Ambition to expand services beyond banking while transitioning into fully digital AI-powered bank

Jaime Augusto Zóbel De Ayala

About Ayala Corporation

Founded in 1834 and headquartered in Makati City, Philippines, Ayala Corp is one of Asia's oldest diversified conglomerates, with the Zóbel family's seventh and eighth generations currently in positions of leadership across the organization, alongside several professional managers and executives

Operates across real estate, banking and financial services, telecommunications, renewable energy, healthcare, education, consumer retail, logistics, and mobility services

Career Highlights and Impact

Chairman and previously CEO of Ayala Corporation; led expansion and diversification since 1994

Pioneered Ayala's entry into telecom (Globe), water infrastructure (Manila Water), renewable energy (ACEN), and healthcare (AC Health)

In 2017, recognized as a UN Sustainable Development Goals pioneer for his work in sustainable business strategy

Ambition to achieve net zero greenhouse gas emissions by 2050 across the entire Ayala Group

Sanjiv Bajaj

About Bajaj Finserv

Holding company for the financial services businesses of the Bajaj Group, one of India's most respected conglomerates with a 100-year legacy

Anchored in building long term, high-quality, sustainable businesses, its three listed entities – Bajaj Finserv, Bajaj Finance, and Bajaj Housing Finance – together have a market capitalization of approximately US$117 billion as of December 2025

Career Highlights and Impact

Managing Director of Bajaj Finserv since 2008 and was appointed as Chairman in 2020

Led the demerger of Bajaj Group financial arm and positioned its companies as India's top lending and insurance businesses. Led digital transformation and adoption of AI for frictionless customer experience, product innovation, and operational excellence

President of the Confederation of Indian Industry (CII), FY 2022–2023

Ambition to reach consolidated PAT of Rs 21,000–Rs 24,000 crore (~US$2.4–2.7 billion) by FY30, implying an 18–22% compound annual growth rate (CAGR) from 2025 levels

Suphachai Chearavanont

About CP (Charoen Pokphand) Group

One of Thailand's largest and most diversified conglomerates, a leading multinational enterprise globally with annual revenues of approximately US$105 billion in 2025

Established in 1921 and headquartered in Bangkok; evolved into a global business with core operations spanning agribusiness and food, retail, and telecommunications across Asia, Europe, and the Americas

Career Highlights and Impact

Senior Vice Chairman of Charoen Pokphand Group

Transformed Thailand's telecom landscape, leading True Corporation to scale its subscriber base to 24 million users during his tenure as CEO

Awarded "Asia Pacific Telecom CEO of the Year" by Frost & Sullivan in 2015

Ambition to achieve net zero carbon emissions by 2050 and significantly reduce carbon emissions by 2030

Wee Ee Cheong

About UOB

Founded in 1935, headquartered in Singapore; a leading Southeast Asian bank with a global network of about 430 branches and offices across 19 countries

Third largest Singapore bank with ~US$572 billion assets and ~US$58 billion market cap as of end 2025

Career Highlights and Impact

Built a bank that advances ASEAN's growth and serves a 650 million population regional economy

Executed the largest acquisition (Citi SEA) in UOB's recent history (~US$3.7 billion)

Over four decades of experience in the financial sector; joined UOB since 1979

Drives long-term impact through a net-zero ambition by 2050 and a sustained commitment to inclusive progress for communities across ASEAN

Seok Cho

About HD Hyundai Electric

Largest share of the US market for ultra-high-capacity transformers (200+ tons) as of early 2025

South Korea–based manufacturer and supplier of electrical and electronic equipment for power generation, transmission, and distribution

Career Highlights and Impact

Currently Vice Chairman of HD Korea Shipbuilding and Offshore Engineering and Chairman of HD Hyundai Group Communications Committee

CEO of HD Hyundai Electric as of late 2019; promoted to Vice Chairman and CEO in 2024

President and CEO of Korea Hydro and Nuclear Power (2013–2016) and Vice Minister for Trade and Energy, Ministry of Knowledge Economy (2011–2013)

Transformed two consecutive years of loss into four straight years of profitability

Ambition to lead HD Hyundai to invest ~US$274 million to increase transformer production capacity by ~30% at Ulsan (Korea) and Alabama (US) plants

Fang Hongbo

About Midea

Founded in 1968, a leading global manufacturer of smart home appliances, HVAC systems, robotics, and industrial automation solutions, serving both consumer and commercial markets

Has 640+ million global consumers, 38 global R&D centers and businesses, expanding to more than 200 countries and regions

Career Highlights and Impact

Joined Midea Group in 1992 and built his career at Midea, succeeding Founder He Xiangjian as Chairman and President in 2012

Architected Midea's core "Global Technology Leadership" strategy, steering the company's landmark transformation from a domestic home appliance manufacturer to a global technology leader in smart home solutions and smart manufacturing

Drove four times revenue expansion under his tenure, putting the company into the Fortune 500 list in 2016, and retaining its global ranking for 10 consecutive years

Orchestrated Midea's full-scale global expansion, broadening the company's worldwide manufacturing and brand footprint and elevating overseas revenue to over 40% of the group's total

Saehong Hur

About GS Caltex

Founded in 1967 and headquartered in Seoul, South Korea, is a major integrated energy and chemical company which operates the world's fourth largest single-site oil refinery

Operations that span petroleum refining, petrochemicals, base oils, and lubricants, supplying a wide range of energy and chemical products to both domestic and global markets

Career Highlights and Impact

CEO of GS Caltex since 2019 and formerly CEO of GS Global from 2017 to 2018; also serves as Chairman of the GS Caltex Board of Directors since 2022 and Vice Chairman of the GS Group since 2026

Led the company's expansion into lower-carbon growth businesses, including biofuels, plastic recycling, hydrogen, and CCUS through industry partnerships and the development of circular resource and clean hydrogen businesses

In 2022, awarded the Order of Industrial Service Merit, Silver Tower by the Government of Korea

In 2025, selected as one of the "100 Centennial Alumni Catalysts" by the Graduate School of Business, Stanford University

Michael B. Kim

About MBK Partners

Asia's largest North Asia private equity (PE) firm with more than US$33 billion AUM (assets under management) as of December 2025

Founded in 2005 and is headquartered in Seoul, South Korea, is the largest independent PE firm focused exclusively on North Asia (Korea, Japan, and China)

Career Highlights and Impact

Founder and Chairman of MBK Partners (2005–present)

Recognized as the "Godfather of Asian PE"; set regional benchmarks for deal size, strategy, and governance

Uday Kotak

About Kotak Mahindra Bank

India's first non-banking financial company to receive a banking license in 2003

Headquartered in Mumbai, India, is a leading private sector bank offering a wide range of banking and financial services

Career Highlights and Impact

Built bank from US$80,000 capital in 1985 to US$47 billion market cap by December 2025

Founded Kotak Mahindra Finance in 1985; transformed it into Kotak Mahindra Bank in 2003

Reinvented the business overnight after the 1992 Indian securities markets scandal affected ~70–75% of revenues

Honored with the Padma Bhushan in January 2026, one of India's highest civilian awards

David Ku

About WeBank

China's first digital-only bank with 1.45 billion daily financial transactions in 2024

Founded in December 2014 and headquartered in Shenzhen, provides a full range of banking services entirely through digital channels without any physical branches

Career Highlights and Impact

Founder and Chairman of WeBank, (2014–present); prior to that, served as a board member of Ping An Group and was a consultant at McKinsey & Company

Transformed banking services for 400 million+ customers using AI, blockchain, cloud, and Big Data

Launched products (Weilidai, Weiyedai) for financial inclusion, serving individuals and mid- and small-sized enterprises

Jeffrey Li

About GL Capital

Leading China healthcare focused PE with more than US$3 billion AUM as of December 2025

Founded in 2010, a PE firm specializing in healthcare, life sciences, and technology investments

Career Highlights and Impact

Country President of Novartis China during 2004–2009

Led US$605 million Nasdaq take-private of SciClone in 2017

Honorary Vice Chairman of China Charity Federation and a member of China Advisory Board of The Nature Conservancy

Ambition to become a global leader in healthcare investment, leveraging its strong foundation in China to expand internationally

Mikhail Lomtadze

About Kaspi

Kazakhstan's first super app with 15.3 million monthly active users (~70% country population)

Kaspi mission is to improve people's lives by developing innovative mobile products and services. Operates a unique two-sided super app model: Kaspi Super App for consumers and Kaspi Pay Super App for merchants

Career Highlights and Impact

CEO and Chief Ecosystem Officer of Kaspi (2007–present); led transformation from a local bank to leading tech super app in Central Asia with ~US$7 billion revenue and ~US$3 billion earnings in 2025

Orchestrated London and NASDAQ initial public offerings (IPOs), putting Kazakhstan on global fintech map

Ambition to expand Kaspi's digital ecosystem beyond Kazakhstan into adjacent high-growth markets. Recently acquired Turkiye's leading e-commerce marketplace Hepsiburada

Sidney Lu

About Foxconn Group/Foxconn Interconnect Technology (FIT)

Foxconn Group founded in 1974 as a plastic parts maker, scaled into the world's leading electronics manufacturer with US$260 billion+ revenue, ~900,000 employees, ranked 28 in Fortune 500 in 2025

Known for its strategic vision, vertical integration, and global expansion, Foxconn Group is one of Taiwan's leading tech companies and a vital part of the global electronics supply chain

Foxconn Group's connector business carved out in 2013 and listed on the Hong Kong Stock Exchange in 2017 as Foxconn Interconnect Technology (FIT)

Career Highlights and Impact

Joined Foxconn in 1990 when the group had US$60 million in revenues; rose from leading a small engineering team to managing the connector and cable business (the *conn* in *Foxconn*, as folklore has it, symbolizing the origins of the Group)

As Chairman and CEO of FIT, has doubled its stock price since FIT's IPO (continuing a legacy of Foxconn Group's ~20% average annual revenue growth over three decades)

Transformed engineering culture by championing the integration of scientific analysis and quality systems – scaling the connector business into Foxconn Interconnect Technology (FIT)

Inducted into 2025 Hall of Fame at University of Illinois Urbana-Champaign (UIUC): established the Tungchao Julia Lu Professorship in his mother's honor (2014), created Sidney Lu Center for Learning and Innovation (2015); university named a building as the Sidney Lu Mechanical Engineering Building in his honor (2019)

Kiran Mazumdar-Shaw

About Biocon

Leading global biopharmaceutical company that develops, manufactures, and commercializes biosimilars, insulins, generic active pharmaceutical ingredients, generic formulations, and novel biologics

India's largest biosimilars company; among top five global biosimilar companies by revenue

Successfully incubated its contract research, development, and manufacturing organization business and unlocked value by listing Syngene in 2015

Career Highlights and Impact

Built one of India's first biotech companies

Founded Biocon in 1978 with ~US$1,200, steering it from industrial enzymes to India's largest biopharma company and global biosimilars leader

Honored with Padma Shri (1989) and Padma Bhushan (2005), two of India's highest civilian awards

Ambition to position Biocon Biologics to capture significant share of the multi-billion-dollar global GLP-1 and insulin market

Anand Mahindra

About Mahindra Group

Founded in 1945 and headquartered in Mumbai, India, is currently a global federation of businesses with more than US$23 billion of revenue and over 350,000 people

Career Highlights and Impact

Transformed from a small steel trading business to a manufacturer of tractors and utility vehicles, to now a leader in automotive (including electric vehicles), farm, financial services, tech services, renewable energy, logistics, real estate, hospitality and other areas

Incisive business commentator and humanitarian with over 11 million followers on X

Honored with the Padma Bhushan in 2020, India's third-highest civilian award. Named in *Barron's* List of Top 30 CEOs worldwide (2016) and *Fortune Magazine*'s list of the World's 50 Greatest Leaders (2014)

Nicholas Moore

About Macquarie

Founded in 1969, headquartered in Sydney; oversaw more than US$620 billion in assets as of December 2025

Global financial services group operating in asset management, retail and business banking, wealth management, advisory, and capital markets

Career Highlights and Impact

CEO and Managing Director, Macquarie Group (2008–2018)

Transformed Macquarie Group during the global financial crisis through strategic risk management, global funds/infrastructure expansion, and diversification

Under his leadership, drove exceptional institutional growth, culminating in assets under management (AUM) exceeding US$550 billion and delivering a 300% increase in shareholder returns by the end of his tenure

Narayana Murthy

About Infosys

Founded in 1981, headquartered in Bengaluru, is the first Indian company listed on NASDAQ (1999)

Global leader in next-generation digital services and consulting, helping clients in ~60 countries navigate digital transformation

Career Highlights and Impact

Led as CEO (1981–2002) and Executive Chairman (2002–2011 and 2013–2014)

Built Infosys from US$250 in startup capital in 1981 to US$20 billion+ in revenues in 2025

Dubbed "Father of the Indian IT sector" by Time and CNBC; pioneered the global delivery model and revolutionized IT outsourcing

Falguni Nayar

About Nykaa

Founded in 2012, is India's leading omnichannel beauty and lifestyle retailer, built on a digital-first, consumer-tech model

The company has scaled to US$1.6 billion gross merchandise value (GMV) and US$50 million EBITDA (FY25), delivering 40%+ five-year GMV CAGR with strong capital efficiency. As of December 2025, serves 52 million customers, operates 276 stores, and offers 9,000+ brands, alongside a fast-growing portfolio of owned labels

Career Highlights and Impact

Led Nykaa's landmark IPO in 2021, making it India's first woman-led unicorn to list within a decade, and one of the few profitable consumer-tech companies at listing

Built Nykaa from first principles into a market-defining company that not only captured demand but also created and formalized India's beauty consumption ecosystem

Led international expansion into the Middle East (Nysaa) and the United Kingdom with India-first foundation vision (partnership with SpaceNK for Kay Beauty)

Akio Nitori

About Nitori Holdings

Japan's largest furniture and home-furnishing retailer with more than 1,000 stores globally

Designs, manufactures, and sells furniture, interior goods, and daily-living products through the Nitori retail chain

Career Highlights and Impact

Founded Nitori in Sapporo in 1967 and grew it into Japan's largest furniture and home-furnishing retailer, leading it for ~60 years; currently serves as Chairman

Led Nitori's expansion globally, with the first store overseas in Taiwan (2007), later in the United States and China, growing to 200+ stores outside Japan

Ambition to reach 3,000 stores globally and achieve ¥3 trillion in sales

Aditya Puri

About HDFC Bank

Founded in 1994 and headquartered in Mumbai, India, is India's largest private sector bank with market capitalization of approximately US$180 billion in 2025

Offers a wide range of financial services, including retail banking, wholesale banking, treasury, and wealth management

Career Highlights and Impact

Founding Managing Director and CEO of HDFC Bank (1994–2020); longest-serving head of any Indian private bank who built India's largest private sector bank by market capitalization

Delivered consistent double-digit profit growth throughout his 26-year tenure (1994–2020)

Built HDFC Bank around India's financial under-penetration, combining foreign bank product capability with domestic scale

Featured on *Barron's* list of top 30 global CEOs: only Indian CEO on the list for fourth consecutive year until 2018

Sarath Ratanavadi

About Gulf Development (Gulf)

Thailand's leading private power producer, with gross installed capacity of ~17.2 gigawatts in February 2026

Focuses on sustainable and innovative energy solutions, including investments in renewable energy and clean power technologies

Career Highlights and Impact

Scaled Gulf from a single IPP project into an energy major (market cap of more than US$20 billion in December 2025)

Led the company's IPO in 2017, one of Thailand's largest corporate IPOs

Awarded the Knight Grand Cross (First Class) of the Order of the Crown of Thailand in 2021, among Thailand's highest royal civilian honors

Ambition to invest US$10 billion in major energy and digital infrastructure globally, concentrating on Thailand

Djohan Emir Setijoso

About Bank Central Asia (BCA)

Founded in 1957, headquartered in Jakarta, Indonesia, is Indonesia's largest bank by market capitalization, ~US$54 billion in 2025

Has an unrivaled transactional network processing 40 billion annual interactions and a disciplined risk framework that yielded a premier 23% return on equity in 2025

Career Highlights and Impact

President Commissioner for PT Bank Central Asia Tbk from 2011 to 2024, providing over a decade of strategic oversight that saw the bank's market capitalization and digital transaction volume reach historic, industry-leading heights

Led the bank through the Asian Financial Crisis, stabilizing liquidity in the face of bank runs and restoring trust in the short term

Built BCA as an independent, enduring institution by restoring trust in employees and the public

Dilip Shanghvi

About Sun Pharma

India's largest pharmaceutical company with market cap of approximately US$45 billion in 2025

Develops, manufactures, and markets a wide range of generic and specialty pharmaceuticals, APIs

Career Highlights and Impact

Founder and Managing Director of Sun Pharma since 1983; Former President of the Indian Pharmaceutical Alliance, former trustee of the Rhodes Scholarship Program at Oxford University

Executed acquisition of Ranbaxy (~US$4 billion) and built India's most valuable healthcare companies

Honored with the Padma Shri in 2016, one of India's highest civilian awards, for his distinguished contribution to the Indian Trade & Industry

Chairman of Sun Pharma Advanced Research Company Ltd., which is engaged in R&D of innovative drugs; Ambition to scale R&D investment to US$1 billion over few years to build a global competitive pipeline

Orchestrated the US$11.75 billion all-cash acquisition of Organon & Co. in 2026, marking the largest-ever acquisition by an Indian pharmaceutical company

Jane Sun

About Trip.com Group

Founded in 1999, Asia's largest online travel agency; offers services including hotel reservations, flight bookings, packaged tours, corporate travel management, and other travel-related services to customers worldwide

Career Highlights and Impact

CEO since 2016, previously serving as CFO (2005–2012) and COO (2012–2015)

Led Trip.com Group's global expansion increasing its market capitalization from ~US$1 billion to ~US$50 billion

International recognition includes

- Fortune's Top 50 Most Powerful Women in Business
- Forbes World's Most Powerful Women and Forbes Asia's Power Businesswomen
- CNBC Changemakers

Ambition to build a dynamic travel ecosystem grounded in shared, sustainable success working closely with partners, destinations, and communities

Takahisa Takahara

About Unicharm

Founded in 1961, headquartered in Tokyo, is a leading Japanese manufacturer of baby care products, feminine care products, wellness care products, and pet care products

Launched world's first "horizontal recycling of disposable diapers"; recycled ~6.7 million diapers as of end of January 2026 instead of being trashed

Career Highlights and Impact

Joined Unicharm in 1984 after university, taking on various roles before becoming president in 2001, president and CEO since 2004

Led Unicharm's global expansion; two-thirds of US$7 billion annual revenue comes from outside Japan

Ambition to contribute to a coexisting society and the achievement of the SDGs, with the goal of becoming number one in global market share by 2030 with a 17% operating profit margin

Itaru Tanimura

About M3

First post-2000 company added to Nikkei 225 (market index for Tokyo Stock Exchange)

Established in September 2000 and headquartered in Tokyo, Japan, is a healthcare-tech company that delivers a wide array of medical-related services via the internet

Career Highlights and Impact

President and CEO of M3, Inc. since September 2000; previously partner at McKinsey & Co.

Led M3's transformation into a global leader in healthcare technology platforms, providing digital solutions to over 6 million physicians and healthcare providers worldwide

Ambition to use internet to increase the number of people who can live longer and healthier lives

Daniel Tsai

About Fubon Group

Founded in 1961, is one of Taiwan's largest conglomerates by total assets (approximately US$400+ billion as of December 2025)

Diversified across financial services, telecommunications, e-commerce, property development, and content businesses – serving the majority of Taiwan's population across every aspect of daily life

Career Highlights and Impact

Joined Fubon in 1981 as part of the founding family leadership and Chairman; co-led its transformation from a mid-sized insurer into one of Taiwan's largest and most profitable financial holding companies

Built Taiwan Mobile into Taiwan's leading private-sector telecom platform (~10 million subscribers, ~30% market share), creating a fully converged mobile, broadband, and digital media ecosystem

Incubated momo.com and transformed it from a TV shopping channel into Taiwan's number one B2C e-commerce platform

Expanded Fubon's holdings outside of Taiwan with major investments in Mainland China, Hong Kong, Vietnam, and South Korea

Honorary Chairman of the Asia Business Council; US$30 million naming gift to Georgetown University Law Center (Daniel Tsai Hall), and a committed long-term champion of children with developmental delays

Joseph Tsai

About Cathay Financial Holdings

Leading financial services group offering insurance, banking, and asset management services in Taiwan with total assets of more than US$450 billion in 2025

Over the last 10 years, Cathay United Bank has built the largest digital banking platform in Taiwan, with currently over 6.8 million users and 47 million logins per month

Career Highlights and Impact

Vice Chairman of Cathay Financial Holdings since mid-2025, and Vice Chairman of Cathay United Bank since 2015

Spearheaded major digital transformation across Cathay Financial's banking and insurance businesses, modernizing customer experience and operational efficiency

Drove Cathay United Bank's strategic expansion in key Asian markets, especially Southeast Asia and China, strengthening the company's regional footprint

About the Authors

Gautam Kumra

Gautam Kumra is the Chairman of McKinsey's offices in Asia, where he is responsible for the firm's performance and health across the region. He previously served on the McKinsey Global Shareholders Council - the firm's highest decision-making body - and has been part of its Global Enablement Team, overseeing the execution of the firm's strategy.

A leading voice on leadership development, Gautam is a Co-founder of the McKinsey Center for CEO Excellence and works closely with CEOs to maximize their effectiveness and support Asian companies in becoming globally competitive institutions.

Over a three-decade career at McKinsey, he has advised leading organizations across Asia and globally on growth strategy, transformation, governance, and leadership, including large-scale change driven by digital and technological shifts.

He has served on several non profit boards, including the Public Health Foundation of India, the IIT Delhi Endowment Board, and the Business Advisory Council of the Lincoln Center for the Performing Arts in New York.

Cheryl Lim

Cheryl Lim is a partner at McKinsey & Company. She is part of the founding leadership team of the McKinsey Center for CEO Excellence, where she helps design and deliver leadership programs for CEOs and senior executives across Asia.

Cheryl is also a global leader in the Firm's People and Organization Performance practice. She advises public and private sector clients on leadership development, talent management, culture change, and operating model transformations to drive growth and enable sustained performance.

With two decades of experience, Cheryl has led large-scale transformations across Asia and the Middle East, helping organizations and systems translate strategy into sustained performance through a deep understanding of organizational effectiveness and health.

Joydeep Sengupta

Joydeep Sengupta is a senior partner at McKinsey & Company, where he founded the McKinsey Center for CEO Excellence and helps CEOs and business leaders transform the performance and health of their organizations.

Joydeep is a member of the McKinsey Global Shareholders Council, the chair of the McKinsey Asia Risk Committee, and member of the Global Client Committee. He has previously led McKinsey's Banking practice as well as the Corporate Finance, Strategy and Organizational practices in Asia.

With nearly three decades of experience in management consulting, Joydeep has extensive expertise in architecting and leading multi-year business transformations across various sectors, especially financial services and digital.

Joydeep also contributes to policy-making groups on financial sector reform and has authored several publications on CEO and board leadership, data and digital banking, and organizational change. He has been a member of multiple Corporate Governance Committees, commissioned by the Reserve Bank of India, and the Securities and Exchange Board of India. Currently he serves on the Corporate Governance Advisory Committee of the Monetary Authority of Singapore.

Notes

Introduction

1. The McKinsey Center for CEO Excellence (MCCE) is McKinsey's dedicated offering for CEO development. The research behind MCCE is based on more than 20 years' worth of data on 7,800 CEOs across 70 countries; it has taught us plenty about the distinctions between the way leaders approach their work.
2. According to the United Nations Economic and Social Commission for Asia and the Pacific (ESCAP): https://www.unescap.org/news/asia-pacific-trade-and-investment-briefs-20245-regional-growth-outperforms-global-average.
3. Defined as US$10,000–$70,000 PPP, as of 2021.
4. ASEAN refers to the Association of Southeast Asian Nations, a political and economic union of 10 countries: Brunei, Cambodia, Indonesia, Laos, Malaysia, Myanmar, the Philippines, Singapore, Thailand, and Vietnam.
5. We focused only on those that appeared in the top 5,000 at least once during 2020–2024.
6. We have three female founders and owner-CEOs featured, which is representative of the number of female CEOs in general. The pool for female CEOs is small to begin with, and the number of female founders even smaller, reflecting the challenges women face from the societal and cultural to the practical, such as access to funding. This roughly tracks global norms: for example, the number of female CEOs leading Fortune 500 companies was 55 in 2025. Source: https://fortune.com/2025/06/02/fortune-500-companies-run-by-female-ceos-women-2025/.

The Influence of Philosophy

1. For more on Kautilya and comparisons with other belief systems, see the work of Devdutt Pattanaik, such as this article from India's *Economic Times*, December 6, 2025, https://devdutt.com/comparing-sun-tzu-and-kautilya/. For more detail on Indian philosophies, consider these sources: https://archive.org/details/httpsierj.injournalindex.phpierjarticleview3008/mode/2up?q=governance, https://ijhit.info/index.php/ijhit/article/view/41/39, and https://www.taylorfrancis.com/chapters/edit/10.4324/9780367808273-5/kautilya-rajarshi-radhakrishnan-pillai.
2. Seok Cho was serving as CEO of HD Hyundai Electric at the time of the interview.

The Influence of History

1. Bata is India's most popular footwear brand and is associated with inexpensive and practical shoes.
2. Biocon was founded in 1978, Infosys in 1981. Reliance Industries dates from 1957, Mahindra & Mahindra from 1945, and Bajaj Group from 1926.
3. Sources: IMF, IAMAI, NPCI.
4. Whereas India's independence happened in 1947, the People's Republic of China was founded under Mao in 1949, who led the country until his death in 1976.

The Power of International Exposure

1. Its beginnings go back to 1921 and the launch of a seed store called Chia Tai Chung in Bangkok's Chinatown.
2. The Taiwanese company Hon Hai Precision operates internationally under the name Foxconn.
3. Foxconn's values in full: Integrity, diligence, agility; share, collaborate, thrive. https://www.honhai.com/en-us/about/core-values.

Catalysts for Restoring Asia's Preeminence

1. In purchasing power parity terms: Asian Development Bank citing Angus Maddison, *Contours of the World Economy 1–2030 AD: Essays in Macro-Economic History* (Oxford University Press, 2007), p. 6. https://www.adb.org/sites/default/files/publication/549191/asias-journey-chapter-1; Asia's Journey to Prosperity - Asian Development Bank.

The Traits That Bind Founders

1. F. Scott Fitzgerald, "The Crack-Up," *Esquire*, February 1936.

Driven by Mission

1. By market capitalization and revenue.

Chapter One: I Am a Pioneer

1. https://www.nitorihd.co.jp/en/.
2. This is the SPA model: sales, production, and purchasing.
3. The article was devised by Anand's grandfather, Jagdish Chandra Mahindra, and Jagdish's younger brother, Kailash Chandra Mahindra. Jagdish became the first iron and steel controller of India during the World War II, while Kailash became head of the India supply mission and was sent to Washington, meeting the founders of International Harvester McCormick and the inventor of the Willys Jeep.

Chapter Three: I Succeed If My Nation and Community Succeed

1. Techcombank's full name is Vietnam Technological and Commercial Joint Stock Bank. It was founded in 1993.
2. The Philippines was colonized by Spain from 1565 to 1898, then the United States from 1898 to 1946, a period interrupted by Japanese occupation during World War II. Full independence came on July 4, 1946.
3. Murthy highlights two, Sri Vittal and Sri Gopalaswamy, who "went out of their way to support our cause."

A Telescope in One Eye, a Microscope in the Other

1. Strictly speaking Macquarie Bank became part of a new holding company structure as Macquarie Group Limited in October 2007.
2. A$43.28 on the Friday before the Lehman bankruptcy announcement, September 12, to A$25.62 on Thursday, September 18. Macquarie's high of this period had been A$97.10 on May 18, 2007; it would eventually bottom out at A$15.75 on March 2, 2009 after falling more than 84% from its high.
3. In February 2021 Macquarie updated guidance on the 2021 financial year. It had previously guided for a year-on-year drop in net profits in the aftermath of the COVID-19 pandemic. Now it suggested it would grow profits by 5–10%, an A$270 million swing, a new record. In the end, Macquarie would report a A$3.015 billion net profit for FY21, up 10% year-on-year. The biggest contribution, of A$2.601 billion, was in commodities and global markets, up 50% year-on-year, with North American Gas and Power mentioned as a key driver. See https://www.macquarie.com/us/en/about/news/2021/macquarie-group-fy21-result-announcement.html.

Chapter Four: I Sense Constantly and Bet on Long-Term Megatrends

1. FY2023 ROE was 32%.
2. ASEAN refers to the Association of Southeast Asian Nations, a political and economic union of 10 countries: Brunei, Cambodia, Indonesia, Laos, Malaysia, Myanmar, the Philippines, Singapore, Thailand, and Vietnam.
3. That's the overall ASEAN population in 2024, not the four markets in which UOB bought. However the population in those four markets is 495 million.
4. Through direct and indirect stakes, the Wee family is estimated to hold more than 20% of the bank (Source: UOB Annual Report).
5. This securities scandal, discussed in more length later in Chapter 5, refers to the 1992 Harshad Mehta incident that led to significant market reforms by the Securities and Exchange Board of India (SEBI).

Chapter Five: I Have No Long Term Without the Short Term

1. https://sustainability.gulf.co.th/en/powering-the-future/decarbonization?
2. https://www.bangkokpost.com/business/general/3060478/gulf-hits-renewable-target-5-years-early.
3. The inclusion of Indonesia's Bank Central Asia, and its president commissioner Djohan Emir Setijoso, in our book warrants some explanation. BCA's origins go back to the 1950s, but like much of the Indonesian banking sector it was taken over during the 1997 Asian financial crisis and placed under a recapitalization program by the Indonesian Bank Restructuring Agency, a state institution. Setijoso was brought in from Bank Rakyat Indonesia in 1999 to rebuild the bank, leading to an initial public offering in 2000, and, subsequently, the sale of a majority stake to another Indonesian family, the Hartonos. So Setijoso is neither the original founder nor part of the controlling dynasty today (the Hartonos) but was effectively the founder-entrepreneur of the reinvented, post-crisis bank.

4. https://www.uobgroup.com/investor-relations/assets/pdfs/investor/financial/2025/news-release-2q-2025.pdf.
5. Market capitalization of US$47 billion in January 2026.
6. https://corporate.m3.com/en/ir/release/2019/pdf/20200312_E_vFF.pdf.

Bold but Bounded

1. Metro Manila population, mid-1990s. In fact 11 million people were to some degree reliant on Metro Manila waterworks.
2. https://www.unescap.org/sites/default/files/Case%202%20-%20Efficiency%20Gains%20-%20Manila%20Water.pdf.
3. The Metropolitan Waterworks and Sewerage System (MWSS).
4. Public-private partnerships, a mainstay structure of private sector participation in infrastructure.
5. Source: Ayala Group.
6. The process of sale to Trident Water Holdings began in 2020 and was concluded in 2024.

Chapter Six: I Align Long-Term Risk with the Scale of Ambition

1. This analysis builds on insights from Chris Bradley, Martin Hirt, and Sven Smit, *Strategy Beyond the Hockey Stick: People, Probabilities, and Big Moves to Beat the Odds* (Wiley, 2018), which identifies five big moves that help companies shift from lower to higher percentiles of economic profit. Two of these moves – pragmatic mergers and acquisitions and disciplined capital expenditure – are used here as proxies to assess the level of risk companies are taking.
2. Reliance Jio Infocomm Limited, to give it its full title, is a subsidiary of Jio Platforms, a holding company for Reliance Jio Infocomm and for other digital businesses of Reliance. Jio Platforms is a subsidiary of Reliance Industries.
3. This was a soft launch with a beta for partners and employees on December 27, 2015. The full launch to the public was on September 5, 2016.

4. Specifically 4G VoLTE, which means Voice over Long-Term Evolution, a system for high-definition voice calls over a data network.
5. They include fiber-to-home, banking, satellite internet, branded smartphones, and numerous multimedia apps across entertainment, health, commerce, and messaging. Jio Payments Bank, a subsidiary of Jio Financial Services and owned by Reliance Industries, has been separately listed since 2023.
6. https://www.icra.in/Rating/GetRationalReportFilePdf/31541~Reliance Jio-R-09122016.pdf, https://www.livemint.com/Companies/DuelrWR275yCA2sWjdrerK/RIL-to-increase-Reliance-Jio-investment-by-Rs15000-crore.html.
7. https://www.livemint.com/market/mark-to-market/zero-to-hero-ril-s-consumer-biz-drives-stock-s-valuation-upgrade-11571858792040.html.
8. https://www.businesstimes.com.sg/companies-markets/ambanis-reliance-spend-us25-billion-5g-across-india.
9. To be precise, Gulf Energy (now Gulf Development) owned a 47.4% stake in Intouch Holdings, which in turn owned a 40.4% stake in AIS. In October 2024 the two companies agreed to merge, with Intouch shareholders approving the merger in March 2025.
10. https://www.pib.gov.in/PressReleasePage.aspx?PRID=2161931.
11. Reliance Industries' market cap was INR18.6 trillion, or US$209.65 billion, on October 7, 2025.
12. Ku's estimates are in line with independent research: https://www.emergenresearch.com/industry-report/digital-assets-market?srsltid=AfmBOoqaSjIlkCPNRtB7L-bDTxMvYqgfayOV7wOs4qGlpFt-xCMoaTwa.
13. https://www.biocon.com/biocon-biologics-to-acquire-viatris-global-biosimilars-assets-in-transformational-deal/.

Chapter Seven: I Move Forward if I Can Live with the Worst Case

1. See slide 10, https://techcombank.com/content/dam/techcombank/public-site/documents/techcombank-6m25-analyst-presentation.pdf.
2. Its generic name is *tildrakizumab*.

Chapter Eight: I Make My Own Luck

1. With considerable success, exports went from 100,000 in 2004 to 600,000 in 2007.
2. https://timesofindia.indiatimes.com/business/india-business/bajaj-finserv-health-to-invest-rs-1000-crore-in-new-direct-to-consumer-health-administration-model/articleshow/115598301.cms.
3. Indian Ministry of Finance, January 31, 2023 citing the Ministry's Economic Survey 2022–3, https://www.pib.gov.in/PressReleasePage.aspx?PRID=1894901.
4. Moore's predecessor, Allan Moss, and Moss's predecessor, Tony Berg, felt the same way. Moore's successor, Shemara Wikramanayake, who joined the bank shortly after him in 1987, articulates the same approach to this day. This may help readers to understand the appearance of Macquarie – not, strictly speaking, a founder-led institution – in this book. There is an extremely clear line of succession through every Macquarie CEO since its foundation, each promoted from within, and in most cases (Berg is the only exception) lifers who stay there until retirement. Furthermore, such is Macquarie's extraordinary level of employee ownership of the stock (Wikramanayake is not thought to have ever sold a single share, and Moore never did in his 32 years at the bank, only after retirement) that it is significantly owned by people who built it.

Chapter Ten: I Look for Opportunities to Disrupt

1. US$47.28 billion equivalent, January 2026.
2. This chart demonstrates it has done so over the long term, though at the end of 2025 the operating margin stood at a lower 22.73%, https://companiesmarketcap.com/sgd/m3/operating-margin/#:~:text=Operating%20Margin%20at%20the%20end,an%20Operating%20Margin%20of%2022.74%25.
3. https://newsable.asianetnews.com/business/foxconn-reports-record-december-q4-and-fullyear-2025-revenue-articleshow-ghv7ui3.
4. 2000 revenues: https://techbreakdowns.substack.com/p/foxconn-founding-story-part-2.
5. 283 million population in 2024 (Source: World Bank).

6. Trip.com Group is the overall company; Trip.com is the international travel brand.
7. Interviewed in 2025.

Chapter Eleven: I Learn from the Best, but Adapt to Make It My Own

1. Industry 4.0 refers to the so-called fourth industrial revolution – fundamentally the use of smart, automated factories using data, artificial intelligence, and the Internet of Things, https://www.mckinsey.com/featured-insights/mckinsey-explainers/what-are-industry-4-0-the-fourth-industrial-revolution-and-4ir.
2. https://www.yicaiglobal.com/news/midea-has-established-a-humanoid-robot-innovation-center-with-the-prototype-being-unveiled-for-first-time, http://english.scio.gov.cn/chinavoices/2025-05/16/content_117878594.html.

Chapter Twelve: I Want Technology to Solve a Real Business Need

1. The "comprehensive digitalization and comprehensive intelligence" strategy launched at the beginning of the pandemic in 2020 delivered clear benefits by 2023, by which time order response speed had improved by 60% and inventory turnover by 35%. In 2024 Midea made intelligence (or "smartization") a core strategic pillar of the group, integrating what it calls the home brain and factory brain with appliances, robots, and solutions. At the company's Jingzhou Factory, an 80% efficiency improvement was achieved. Overall, Midea's cumulative research and development (R&D) investment is over RMB100 billion in a decade, and RMB13 billion in 2023 alone; consistently more than 3.5% total revenue is spent on R&D.

Chapter Fourteen: I Develop People Through Stretch Opportunities

1. No. 1 for liberal arts major students in the MyNavi/Nikkei ranking of the most popular companies for university students, 2024 and 2025; no. 1 in the overall category in the Rakuten Minshu Internship ranking of the most popular companies (five consecutive years from 2019).
2. https://www.nitorihd.co.jp/en/about_us/corporate_data.html.
3. Bajaj Allianz General Insurance (BAGIG) and Bajaj Allianz Life Insurance (BALIC).

Chapter Fifteen: I Take a Through-Cycle Approach to People

1. https://www.ril.com/ar2023-24/human-capital.html.
2. https://careers.ril.com/rilcareers/frmemployeebenefitsN.aspx.
3. He has sold some since leaving Macquarie.
4. https://www.afr.com/markets/shemara-wikramanayake-has-never-sold-a-macquarie-share-in-30-years-20171204-gzy8bh.

Scale Without Losing Soul

1. https://www.midea.com/in/about-midea.
2. Midea today operates through five major sectors: smart home, new energy and industrial technology, building technologies, robotics and automation, and innovative businesses.

Chapter Sixteen: I Want to Preserve My Entrepreneurial Core

1. https://www.mckinsey.com/capabilities/people-and-organizational-performance/our-insights/achieving-hypergrowth-its-all-about-the-people.
2. https://www.mckinsey.com/capabilities/people-and-organizational-performance/our-insights/from-start-up-to-centaur-leadership-lessons-on-scaling.
3. India has a population of 1.45 billion, China 1.4 billion, Indonesia 285 million, Pakistan 255 million. Bangladesh, Japan, the Philippines, and Vietnam each have over 100 million, https://www.unfpa.org/data/world-population-dashboard.
4. Asia and the Pacific accounted for 38.9% of global nominal exports in 2024, the highest bloc in the world, https://repository.unescap.org/server/api/core/bitstreams/43cb1e18-f351-4ff4-b251-e20ac27bf885/content.
5. https://techcombank.com/en/investors/annual-report/2023/corporate-culture.
6. https://www.ibtimes.co.in/infosys-split-business-into-smaller-units-says-ceo-vishal-sikka-691620.
7. https://www.infosys.com/newsroom/press-releases/Documents/2000/Mohali-10Mar00.pdf.

Chapter Seventeen: I Strive to Manage Business Transition and Family

1. https://www.philstar.com/business/2012/03/18/787816/zóbel-family-council-ensuring-next-generation-leaders.
2. See Forbes.com, "Pharma Billionaire Dilip Shanghvi Positions Next Gen for Succession," October 8, 2025.
3. Acha Leke, Avinash Goyal, and Chaitali Mukherjee, Passing the baton effectively: CEO succession at family-owned businesses, McKinsey & Company, February 2026, https://www.mckinsey.com/industries/private-capital/our-insights/passing-the-baton-creating-value-through-ceo-succession-at-family-businesses.
4. Leke, Goyal, and Mukherjee, "Passing the Baton Effectively."

Chapter Eighteen: I Build an Institution That Outlives Me

1. See Sven Smit and Gemma D'Auria's Corporate longevity: Business and org practices that matter most.

Index

INDEX